Trees of
Greater Portland

A view of the South Park Blocks from Clay St. 5-19-91.

Trees of
Greater Portland

Phyllis C. Reynolds

and

Elizabeth F. Dimon

TIMBER PRESS
Portland, Oregon

ISBN 0-88192-263-3
Printed in Hong Kong

TIMBER PRESS, INC.
9999 S.W. Wilshire, Suite 124
Portland, Oregon 97225

Library of Congress Cataloging-in-Publication Data

Reynolds, Phyllis C.
    Trees of greater Portland / Phyllis C. Reynolds and Elizabeth F.
Dimon.
        p.   cm.
    Includes bibliographical references and index.
    ISBN 0-88192-263-3
    1. Trees in cities--Oregon--Portland Metropolitan Area-
-Guidebooks. 2. Trees--Oregon--Portland Metropolitan Area-
-Identification. 3. Portland Metropolitan Area (Or.)--Guidebooks.
I. Dimon, Elizabeth F.   II. Title.
SB435.52.072P677 1993
635.9'77'0979549--dc20   92-19585
                                                    CIP

Dedication

On 13 November 1991, before this book went to press, Elizabeth Dimon died suddenly and unexpectedly of a heart attack. I should like to make this book a memorial to her—a salute to the many, many hours we spent together working over *Trees of Greater Portland*. Elizabeth loved and cherished trees—I remember so well her anger and sadness when she saw a big, old beauty chopped to the ground. So here's to you, my friend, in hope that this book will keep many big, old beauties alive.

Contents

Preface. 9
Acknowledgments. 13
Introduction 15
Descriptions 23
Appendix A: Best Tree Viewing Times. 175
Appendix B: Nine Tree Tours. 181
Appendix C: Largest Trees 201
Selected Bibliography. 203
Glossary 205
Index of Tree Names 209
About the Authors 215

Preface

We do not remember the exact moment the idea for this book was conceived. In the beginning we drove around town looking for the trees on Bill (Robbie) Robinson's list from the 1970s. We soon discovered that many trees on that list no longer existed. Were they dead from old age? Had someone chopped them down? Who knows? The more we cruised, the more we realized that other notable trees were out there. The moment of conception must have occurred early in 1989 when one of us said, "These trees need to be in a book," and the other agreed.

We began our serious work by searching for street trees that have significance because of their age, historical background, form and beauty, or rarity. Knowing that some big beauties were outside Portland's legal boundaries, we chose to include much of the Greater Portland area: Sauvie Island, Gresham, Oregon City, Tigard, and Beaverton, encompassing about 350 square miles and portions of three counties (Multnomah, Clackamas, and Washington). It was impossible to cover this large area block by block. In fact, there are neighborhoods that we do not know well enough, and we have probably missed some significant trees. We apologize if we have omitted an obvious candidate and invite readers with knowledge of a special street tree to contact us. Historical facts, too, are always welcome.

This book is not primarily a tree identification book. For the most part, it presents a photograph to help readers identify a particular noteworthy tree. Once readers see the tree, they can inspect it so they can identify the same type of tree when they see it elsewhere. Frequently the species descriptions in this volume include a close-up photograph of an identifying aspect of the tree (e.g., the fruit, the leaf). Occasionally the photograph of an enormous tree had to be taken at such a distance that individual features, such as leaf length and blossom size, are too obscure. In these cases the close-up photograph will help readers.

Many trees have cultivar names in addition to their designated species name. It is often very difficult to determine accurate cultivar names, and we have not, for the most part, identified a tree by this name. Readers who are interested in these fine details should visit a tree nursery, or consult a reference book. Those readers who want to know what street trees (often cultivars) are recommended by Portland's Forestry Division can visit the division's experimental plot in East Delta Park. Stop at the office, open Monday through Friday from 7:00 A.M. to 3:30 P.M., to get a map showing the location of the trees.

Many of the photographs in this guide show overhead wires, telephone poles, automobiles, or people. This is because every tree in the book is either a street tree or one that can be easily viewed from the street. Many more trees could have been included except that they are not visible from a public street. Only two trees—one an old apple tree of historical significance and the other the largest bigleaf maple in town—are approached by a short nonpublic road. The developer of the residential area where the apple tree is located has left the tree standing and the Home Orchard Society has added a plaque to be viewed by the public. We therefore feel that, although the road is designated as "private," the public can either drive or walk the short distance to see this remarkable specimen. Another tree, a copper beech at Portland State University, is on public land but must be approached by foot.

Occasionally the biggest tree we found is one that simply could not be photographed, although its massive size can be viewed clearly from the street. An example is a *Sequoiadendron giganteum* (giant sequoia) in the Mount Tabor area. The *Sequoiadendron* photographs in this book are of trees of lesser stature that could be adequately photographed. Once readers see the distinct conical shape of this species, they will have no difficulty spotting it, often towering above all other trees, throughout the metropolitan area. Many giant sequoias have been planted over the years and poke up their sharp heads in the city.

In the process of taking photographs for this volume, we became partial to certain trees, most of them natives—*Arbutus menziesii* (Pacific madrone), *Cornus nuttallii* (Pacific dogwood), *Quercus garryana* (Garry or Oregon white oak), and *Pinus ponderosa* (ponderosa pine). These species are so beautiful we were carried away with photographing them. Readers will see the product of our enthusiasm in this book as it became too difficult for us to choose one representative photograph.

We have compiled this book with the Saturday stroller, the everyday bicyclist, and the Sunday driver in mind. Each species description includes the location of a notable tree (usually the street address), a photograph with the date the photograph was taken, and, when possible, the location of at least one other tree of the same taxon in another part of town. We do not intend to be exhaustive or inclusive in the listings of additional specimens; we include the addresses primarily for the readers' convenience. For trees outside Portland proper, we indicate the city or town in which they grow (e.g., Beaverton, Oregon City). The description includes data on the tree's historical significance (if any), the date it was planted, the name of the planter (if known), and a few characteristics of the taxon.

In many instances the description includes both the circumference and the diameter of the tree. If these measurements are missing, it is because a fence or a dog kept us away or because the information is not significant for a particular tree. Property owners and city forestry departments often trim trees, making height and crown spread unreliable measurements for estimating tree size, and very often we could not measure the crown spread anyway because it would have meant risking our lives to attain a measurement in the middle of a busy street. Therefore, circumference (or diameter) gives the best overall estimate of the size of a city tree. When measuring tree circumference, we followed the measurement procedure of the American Forestry Association as outlined in an undated pamphlet titled *National Register of Big Trees:*

> The circumference of the tree is measured at 4½ feet above the center of the base of the tree. If the trunk has a growth or branch at that height or below, the circumference is measured in feet and inches at the point below 4½ feet where the circumference is least. If the ground is not level at the base of the trunk, take an average at 4½ feet.

For a few species in the book the reader will find a measurement for the largest tree in Oregon. These data are maintained by the National Register of Big Trees. Once a tree is identified and measured (girth, height, and crown), it is measured again only if a challenger tree is found. Hence, some of the dates of measurement are over 20 years old.

For clarity and precision, the trees in this volume are listed alphabetically by botanic name, starting with *Abies* and ending with *Zelkova*. To assist readers who may be nervous about pronouncing botanic names, an easy guide to pronounciation immediately follows each name. The common name(s) of the tree is(are) also given, and both botanic and common names are listed in the index. Our primary reference for names in this book is *Hortus Third.*

Appendix A groups trees by season to indicate the best viewing times. For those interested in viewing a good collection of notable trees within a relatively small area, Appendix B provides seven tree tours for strollers and two for Sunday drivers or bicyclists. Appendix

C lists the largest trees described in this book.

The Portland metropolitan area has many beautiful parks that contain outstanding examples of numerous species of trees. For the most part these trees have not been included in this book, primarily because they cannot be seen from the street. We encourage readers to visit the parks to look at the trees. In Hoyt Arboretum, for example, all the trees are labelled, and visitors can purchase maps and a guide to tree location. The arboretum also has miles of hiking trails.

Finally, we urge readers to remember that many of the trees in this book are on private property. Please do not trespass. It was gratifying to us that virtually all the tree owners we contacted were willing and eager to share their trees with the public.

And now, we hope you enjoy Greater Portland's beautiful and notable trees as much as we have. We are, indeed, a fortunate city!

Acknowledgments

We want to thank all our friends who were so helpful in telling us about special trees here and there. And, we have a rather long list of persons who deserve our deep gratitude for their assistance in various ways: Mary Ann Casson, Pearl Costa, Peggy Glasscock, Ruth Hansen, Bill Hawkins, Craig Jensen, Florence Lehman, Scott Mayer, Christa McDonald, Brian McInerny, Mike Mosher, Fred Nilsen, Oregon Historical Society librarians, Robbie Robinson, Bill Sauerwein, Jill Schatz, Joan Smith, Nadine Smith, Sue Thomas, Inez Oatfield West, Alex Wynstra, and Harry Zimmerman. Our very special thanks to Stan Lindstrom and Avory Gray who gave us, without complaint, many hours of their expertise; the book in its present form would not exist without them. Finally, our thanks to our publisher, Bob Conklin, who believed in us, and to our editor, Linda Willms, who expertly shepherded us to the end.

Introduction

How green is our valley! Perhaps we take it for granted, surrounded as we are by lofty second-growth firs, majestic maples, and myriad other varieties, but our vast stands of timber and luxuriant garden trees, which are among our greatest scenic assets in the Willamette Valley, continue to impress our visitors. For more than one hundred and fifty years, landscapers, gardeners, and city planners have taken advantage of the ideal growing conditions here—a temperate climate, deep soils, and, most certainly, ample water. Between 150 and 175 different species of trees grow well in the Willamette Valley; of the 48 species native to Oregon, 22 are native to the Greater Portland area.

Eons before Native Americans arrived, and even after, the area that is now Greater Portland was a boreal, mesic conifer forest. The dominant species was Douglas fir (*Pseudotsuga menziesii*), with vine maple (*Acer circinatum*), bigleaf maple (*Acer macrophyllum*), Western hazel (*Corylus cornuta*), and Oregon white oak (*Quercus garryana*) all well represented. The most common understory plants were salal (*Gaultheria shallon*), Oregon grape (*Mahonia aquifolium*), and sword fern (*Polystichum munitum*). Early explorers noted our native fruits as well: Oregon crabapple (*Pyrus fusca*), Indian plum (*Oemlaria cerasiformis*), wild cherry (*Prunus emarginata* var. *mollis*), elderberries (*Sambucus cerulea* and *S. racemosa*), hawthorn (*Crataegus douglasii*), and golden chinquapin (*Castanopsis chrysophylla*).

Tree lovers ranging from druids to woodchoppers have been in Oregon since it was first inhabited. The true tree addict always focuses his or her attention admiringly skyward or sideways—seldom on the road ahead. The true woodchopper views the same trees, but sees and measures them only in terms of financial gain, board feet, or development potential. In Portland's early days, the woodchoppers prevailed. It was fundamental to clear the land to be occupied by the incoming waves of settlers from the East. By 1845, four streets and 16 blocks along the Willamette River had been cleared, and later that year the fledgling town was officially named

"Portland" by the toss of a coin in Oregon City.

Many of the trees that were cut down left sizeable stumps that remained in place, for, as anyone who has tried knows, grubbing out stumps requires long, tedious, back-breaking effort. Thus, despite the official name, travelers passing by on the river promptly dubbed the settlement "Stumptown." The stumps in Portland's first streets were whitewashed to prevent late-night collisions by pedestrians. Some old houses were even built on very large stumps that served as footings.

By the 1840s lumber was needed for the buildings that began to fill the cleared land, a need that continues to this day. There were plank buildings, plank sidewalks, and even the Great Plank Road to the Tualatin Valley. Logs were used for pilings and slabwood-fueled furnaces, steamboats, and later, railroad steam engines. The closest and handiest trees succumbed most readily to the new sawmills, and by the 1870s, photos of the West Hills showed the effects of this deforestation. With the needs of local settlers more than met, enormous log rafts containing thousands of trees were floated to ports in California as well.

In this population of woodchoppers there were also a few far-sighted individuals who appreciated the form, size, and massive bulk of outstanding trees. They were the citizens who began to set aside parks and plant young trees, not only for fruit or nuts, but also for beauty.

All accounts of tree planting in this area begin with an employee of the Hudson's Bay Trading Company, who carried apple seeds in his vest pocket from London to Fort Vancouver in 1824. These seeds were delivered to the appointed Fort Vancouver gardener, James Bruce, for planting. An 1833 report describes the fort's 700-acre farm, which included peach and apple orchards, and three years later Narcissa Whitman wrote that the farm grew fruits of every description.

Another report mentions grafted fruit trees at Wapatoo (Sauvie) Island in 1835, which must have been carried from the Sandwich Islands to Captain Nathaniel Wyeth's short-lived settlement, Fort William. In 1845 Gustavus Hines wrote:

> Apples, peaches, and other kinds of fruit flourish as far as they have been cultivated; and from present appearances, it is quite likely that the time is not far distant when the country will be well-supplied with the various kinds of fruit which grow in the Middle States (Workers of the Writer's Program of the WPA 1940, 54).

Some pioneering families carried seeds in their wagons for a small orchard, but larger collections were either lost or thrown away—until 1847. In that year, Henderson Luelling and his party carried nursery stock from Iowa to Oregon in specially constructed wagons. The well-planned trip, which was undertaken as a business venture, introduced most of the named fruit varieties of the time to Oregon. Luelling planted his trees on a 640-acre Donation Land Claim (DLC) to the north of Milwaukie, where the Waverley Country Club now stands, and thus the nursery business began in Oregon. With the DLCs of Luelling's son-in-law William Meek and son Alfred, the family ran a sizeable enterprise on the east bank of the Willamette. Ralph C. Geer, who crossed the plains in the same year, brought a bushel of apple seeds and a half-bushel of pear seeds. He set them out in the Waldo Hills near Salem and supplied rootstock for Luelling, who in turn gave Geer buds from the wagonload of nursery trees.

The popularity of the young trees raised from Luelling's wagonload was immediate. One of Portland's earliest and best-known tree lovers, Dr. James Robert Cardwell, reported:

> It is said of some of the earliest settlers in the Willamette Valley that nothing more thoroughly and painfully accentuated their isolated conditions than the absence of fruit trees on their newly-made farms. . . . People in those days knew what their neighbors were doing, and in the fall of 1848 they came from hundreds of miles from all over the country for scions and young trees to set in their little dooryard or to start an orchard; so that the trees were soon distributed all over the settlements of the valley—yearlings selling at fifty cents to one dollar each (Cardwell 1906, 7, 10).

In 1850 Luelling returned east and imported across the Isthmus of Panama a large variety of young trees. No documentation exists of their names, but they were selected from Ellwanger and Barry, and A. J. Downing in New York. In the same year J. W. Ladd started a nursery near Butteville listing fruit, shrubbery, and ornamental trees. George Settlemier arrived by way of California in 1850 with a good supply of fruit tree seeds that he planted and later removed to his home at Mt. Angel, where "as fast as his limited means would allow, a large stock of fruit and ornamental trees were accumulated, making in all the largest variety in the Territory." His son, J. H. Settlemier, started the famous Settlemier nursery in Woodburn in 1863. Others setting orchards included P. F. Bradford, Dr. O. P. S. Plummer, S. A. Clarke, George Walling, Dr. N. G. Blalock, Henry and David Prettyman, Daniel Brock, and Henry E. Dosch. These pioneers found a ready market in the constant influx of new citizens to the Portland area.

In 1857 the growers formed an organization later known as the Oregon State Agricultural Society. Members were George and Albert Walling from Oswego; Henry Miller, Joseph Lambert, and Seth Lewelling from Milwaukie; James B. Stephens from East Portland; Henry Prettyman from Mount Tabor; J. A. Settlemier from Woodburn; Thomas Frazier and John Minto from Salem. In October 1861 this group sponsored a state fair in Gladstone. Today, the ancient Pow-wow Maple marks the location of the entrance gate to that vanished fairground.

Among the first nursery owners to market trees for their ornamental use were Percy W. Gillette in Astoria, Henderson Luelling and his brother Seth (who chose to spell his name Lewelling), and Joseph Lambert and his father-in-law Henry Miller. Lambert and Miller bought the Luelling DLC from William Meek in 1859 and took over the Waverley farm. Henderson moved on to California after only seven years in Oregon, leaving Seth in Milwaukie to become the horticulturist in the family. Great-granddaughter Janie L. Byrnes (personal communication 1979) summed it up this way: "Uncle Seth settled down and developed new varieties while Grampa Henderson just went around scattering nurseries here and there."

For many years Milwaukie was the center of Oregon's nursery business. Seth Lewelling developed the Bing cherry there in the 1870s. Joseph Lambert propagated the 'Lambert' and other cherries on the Waverley farm. Henry Miller, whose interest was ornamentals, built greenhouses on the farm to propagate some new-to-the-area varieties. An early Miller invoice lists the following medley of plants that were purchased by Mrs. Frank Kerr: bamboo, apple trees, cherries, figs, filberts, ginkgos, double scarlet hawthorn, various forms of holly, and a white horsechestnut.

As ornamentals were propagated and became available for distribution, pleasure gardens began to take shape around the settlers' homes, and, to the degree the houses became more elaborate in Victorian years, so did the surrounding gardens. Trees were imported from the Orient, the East, and Europe, and the charming, small specimens of little-known species became, with the passage of time, skyline landmarks.

In 1871 Henry Miller moved his greenhouses and his home from Milwaukie to a tract of land on upper Jefferson Street, which bordered the Great Plank Road to the Tualatin Valley. Judge O. N. Denny, consul to China and advisor to the king of Korea, sent Miller plants from the Orient, among them the first camellias and magnolias. Soon pink dogwoods lined Miller's drive, and his garden was described as one of the most beautiful properties in Oregon. From it, Miller sold camellia blossoms and became known as Portland's first florist. A few of the large, old trees that remain—a 120-year-old cedar of Lebanon and an Austrian pine—have been proposed for historic status as documented specimens belonging to an outstanding horticultural pioneer in Portland.

Legend has it that Portland's giant sequoias were planted as bench markers in the early days, but today they are so numerous they would only confuse a surveyor. Who planted them and which were the marker sequoias? No one knows for certain. Perhaps it was Colonel Lester Leander Hawkins, a surveyor and banker, who brought cones from sequoias in Yosemite and gave young seedling trees to some of his friends. Perhaps it was John Broetje, who planted sequoias thickly in the Oak Grove area south of Milwaukie in the late 1800s after moving his nursery from the end of Hawthorne Street in the Mount Tabor area. Or perhaps it was John R. Porter, who arrived in 1869 from California with two gunny sacks of *Sequoiadendron giganteum* seeds, which he planted at his nursery near Verboort. The seedlings were sold throughout what is now Washington County.

The Lewis and Clark Exposition in 1905 introduced several exotics to Portland, such as rhododendron, yucca, and varieties of bamboo. The South American building dispensed *Araucaria araucana* (monkey puzzle trees).

Very early in Portland's history (1852) land was set aside for what are now known as the Plaza and Park Blocks: "This avenue is indispensable for all classes of our population," wrote *The Oregonian* in 1871. "Planted with trees . . . [these blocks] would be a pride to the city and a source of gladness and health." Shortly thereafter, in 1871, City Park, which is today known as Washington Park, was created. Now comprising about 100 acres, it contains, among other things, thousands of big, old trees.

In 1903 John Charles Olmsted, son of Frederick Law Olmsted of New York's Central Park renown, came to Portland on behalf of the Olmsted Bros. firm to assist the city in laying out a plan of parks. At the time the West Side had two parks of considerable size, while the East Side had only one larger than a square: Columbia Park. Colonel Lester Leander Hawkins of the Park Commission drove Olmsted about the city "preparing [his] mind for this duty." Provided with maps, Olmsted took numerous photographs. Many of the firm's suggestions and improvements were acted upon and the summary of its report, "Outlining a System of Parkways, Boulevards and Parks," dated 31 December 1903, is interesting reading indeed.

The history of trees in the Portland area is, then, a history of the people and groups who planned for them, planted them, cared for them, protected them, and publicized them. Besides those already mentioned, there are others such as Colburn Barrell, who brought an elm, later known as the Washington Elm, in a keg from his Massachusetts home. Albert Weisendanger, director of Keep Oregon Green, was the forest ranger who found the imprints of the fossil ginkgos about 1925. Bill (Robbie) Robinson compiled a base list of Portland's notable and historic trees in 1974 and is personally respon-sible for the recognition and preservation of several trees. Maynard Drawson is still occupied with scouting out trees of record size and preserving notable ones throughout the state. Dr. J. R. Cardwell, who "had the tree-setting craze and had it bad," has an equal today in Stan Lindstrom, who never met a tree he did not know. Larry McGraw planted the pioneer orchard on Sauvie Island, which is maintained by the Home Orchard Society. Friends of Trees is a new citizen group involved with planting trees and recording historic ones. Thus, from David Douglas and Thomas Nuttall, who was based at Wyeth's Fort William in the 1830s, to the curators of the Hoyt Arboretum and the founders of the city's botanic gardens, Portland continues to attract tree people of the finest order.

One such person is Alex Wynstra, the city of Portland's forester, who started the Urban Forestry Division in 1974 and has saved hundreds of trees from an early demise. In 1991 the Forestry division was responsible for 2000 miles of street trees and 9600 acres of park trees. According to Section 20.40.150 of the the city's tree ordinance, the city forester is also responsible for maintaining a list of historically significant trees:

Historic or notable trees: The Forester will . . . prepare a list of trees within the city which, because of their age, type, notability or historical association are of special importance. Upon recommendation of the Historic Landmarks Commission and the approval of the City Council, such a tree will be designated an "Historic Tree." . . . An historic tree may not be removed without a public hearing before the Commission at least 30 days prior to the proposed date of removal. This chapter of the ordinance does hereby give full and complete authority to the Forester over any and all historic trees in the City.

Wynstra hopes the ordinance will be revised to require the consent of property owners on whose land threatened, significant trees are located. He foresees financial problems as more and more historic and notable trees are so identified. It is sad that trees identified as historic, and thereby under the surveillance of the city forester, are not funded. To properly care for trees on private lands, it may be necessary to set up a private fund.

Other ordinances protect small woodlots (by forbidding the harvest of trees within the city boundaries on lots 2 acres or larger), regulate solar-friendly qualities of a tree, proclaim that trees infested with Dutch elm disease are a public nuisance, and regulate selection of replacement trees. A 1982 city council record encourages homeowners to plant trees:

For environmental and aesthetic reasons, street trees in urban core areas are appropriate and beneficial additions to the streetscape. . . . Tree permits are issued according to a fee schedule based on the value of improvements.

Other cities in the Greater Portland area approach the care and maintenance of their tree populations with varying degrees of interest. Pressure for increased development in Lake Oswego has long been a cause for concern among the tree people there. Several years ago, a tree walk in the downtown area was defined on a map and specimen trees were marked with identifying signs. Since then, however, many trees and/or signs have been lost for one reason or another. The city plans to toughen the criteria for obtaining a tree-cutting permit. Beaverton has a well-established, comprehensive program of tree preservation, complete with photographs and a well-defined map, updated as needed, of historic trees and groves. Although Oregon City maintains a list of historic houses that are well preserved, it does not have a list of historic trees, protected or otherwise. Individual specimens have been set aside by various groups, but the code enforces only clearances. Milwaukie's present-day tree ordinance merely provides for a 12-foot clearance above the right-of-way for passing vehicles. Ron Pomeroy, with the Tigard Planning Department, characterizes his city as fairly conservative regarding the removal of trees. New development areas are personally checked to see that root compaction is avoided and all possible trees are retained. In Gresham, citizens spoke up early in the 1970s to protect the stand of Hogan cedars threatened by the routing of the proposed Mount Hood freeway. In early 1991 the city enacted a tree preservation ordinance that provides for the protection of "significant trees" and limits the number of large trees that may be removed from any site. An inventory of significant trees now exists.

Many of the areas surrounding the city proper have not yet faced the development pressures of the suburbs and, consequently, still boast wonderful examples of large, old trees. Farm roads built last century between communities, such as the roads between Gresham and Portland, Portland and Oregon City, the Great Plank Road (now Canyon Road, for the most part), Capitol Highway, the "Ferry" roads, the Beaverton-Hillsdale Highway, and other early paths of commerce, are often bordered with pioneer trees.

Public support is crucial to the well-being of fine trees. Many of the trees described in this book are survivors—of the hurricane winds in the Columbus Day storm of 1962 (when Portland alone lost over 16,000 trees), of pests, or of the pressures of civilization. Urban trees in particular face threats throughout their lives from development, harsh growing conditions, and ignorance. In fact, when the idea of new street trees was proposed for downtown Portland in the 1950s, it was thought the trees would thrive tucked into pots, a notion that quickly proved unsuccessful.

Benign neglect may be the best policy for those areas that have been cleared. Open space, if undisturbed, will be reforested by birds, squirrels, and winds. They scatter the seeds, not only of our native plants but of solidly established imports. Citizen groups that plant a tree to cool the globe, as instructed by the American Forestry Association, may inadvertently introduce a variety that is ecologically inappropriate. A field is better left fallow to reforest itself with species already adapted to Oregon. Recognizing and learning more about the existing elements of Greater Portland's greenery would naturally lead to better choices, an increased understanding, and greater friendship with the trees.

Descriptions

The following abbreviations are used:

    c = circumference
    d = diameter
    NT = next to
    X = across the street from

Abies concolor

(ā-bēz *kon*-kul-er)

White fir
Evergreen

Abies concolor, White fir. 2156 SW Laurel St. 7-1-91. 6′ c, 1′11″ d. The gray-blue needles show up well against the dark green of the Norway spruce. Two sawara cypresses are in the foreground and a Norway spruce is behind.

A tree with beautiful gray-blue foliage, the white fir is a native of central and northeast Oregon, the southern Cascades, California, Arizona, and New Mexico. Compared to many other true firs, its needles are long (up to 3 inches). Growing to 100 feet or more in height and 2 to 4 feet in diameter in the city, this fir can reach 250 feet high with a diameter of over 6 feet in the wild. It naturally occurs at low elevations and in soil tending to be dry. In gardens it withstands drought, heat, and cold.

Few white firs grow in the Portland area. Because of its foliage color some people mistake it for a blue Colorado spruce.

- 812 NE 53rd Ave., 5′8″ c, 1′10″ d
- 3326 NE Couch St.
- 1733 N Alberta St.
- 2126 NE Regents Dr.
- 2865 SW Fairview Blvd.
- 9312 SE 29th Ave, Milwaukie

Abies grandis, Grand fir. SW Fairview Blvd. & Knights Rd., Hoyt Arboretum. 3-8-91. 7'4" c, 2'4" d. Planted 1936.

Abies grandis

(ā-bēz *grand*-iss)

Grand fir
Evergreen

This tree can be found in the Pacific Northwest at lower elevations west of the Cascades, and up to 6000 feet in Idaho. Its rather long needles (up to 2.25 inches) are shiny dark green above and whitish on the underside. The needles spread in two regular, comblike rows from opposite sides of the branchlet. The tree can attain huge dimensions: 200 feet in height and 5 feet in diameter. Scottish botanist David Douglas discovered this fir and first cultivated it in 1830.

Although native to Portland, few grand firs remain along urban neighborhood streets.

- SW Sacajawea Blvd., Washington Park, 13'11" c, 4'5" d (an enormous tree with a missing middle and top)
- NT 811 SE Sherrett St., 8' c, 2'7" d

Abies pinsapo

(ā-bēz pin-*sa*-po)

Spanish fir
Evergreen

Abies pinsapo, Spanish fir. 9008 N Charleston Ave. 3-15-90. 8′ c, 2′6″ d.

Because of its short, stiff, sharp leaves emerging at right angles from the branch, this tree has been called the "hedgehog fir." Its needles grow all around the branch, in contrast to any other true fir. With a small native range in the mountains of southern Spain, it can attain a height of about 80 feet. Superficially this tree looks like a spruce, but its lavender-brown cones, which stand up on the branch like fat candles, reveal it as a true fir. The cones do not drop off the tree intact but disintegrate scale by scale, leaving the woody axis on the branch looking like a spindle.

- 2060 NE 238th Ave., Wood Village, 7′5″ c, 2′4″ d
- 3181 SW Sam Jackson Park Rd., 6′5″ c, 2′ d (not visible from the street but may be reached by walking behind Baird Hall)
- corner NE 65th Ave. & Davis St., 5′6″ c, 1′9″ d
- corner SE 4th Ave. & Stark St., 5′5″ c, 1′9″ d
- X 3908 NE Couch St., 5′ c, 1′7″ d

Abies pinsapo, Spanish fir. 3-8-91.

Abies procera

(ā-bēz prō-*ser*-a)

Noble fir
Evergreen

Abies procera, Noble fir. 5225 N Concord Ave. 4-11-91. 6'9" c, 2'2" d.

One of Oregon's native trees, the noble fir's habitat is the western slopes of the Cascades as far west as Larch Mountain in the Columbia Gorge. Its companions are Douglas firs, Western hemlocks, and occasionally Pacific silver firs. In the wild this fir reaches impressive heights of over 300 feet and typically has a slightly rounded crown and branches that are stiffly horizontal. Its needles, which resemble small hockey sticks as they emerge from the branch, have a marvelous fragrance. This species is often used as a Christmas tree. In 1830 Scottish explorer-botanist David Douglas collected seeds of this fir in the Cascades and wrote: "I spent three weeks in a forest composed of this tree, and day by day could not cease to admire it" (quoted in Davies 1980, 153).

The biggest and best noble firs in town grow at Hoyt Arboretum, at some distance from a road.

- 1710 N Humboldt St., 7'9" c, 2'6" d
- 1732 N Alberta St.

Acer campestre, Hedge or Field maple. 2577 NE Mult-nomah St. 5-19-90. 9'5" c, 3' d. Two specimens, believed to be the largest in Portland, one year after a severe pruning.

Acer campestre

(ā-ser kam-*pes*-tre)

Hedge or Field maple
Deciduous

Native over the greater part of Europe, from Great Britain and Sweden as far as Iran in western Asia, this maple is a slow grower, usually attaining a height of no more than 65 feet; more often it can be seen in the 35-foot range. It naturally has a rounded head. The seeds are 1–1.5 inches long and the wings diverge horizontally with no narrowing toward the base. Like the Norway maple, leaf stalks of the hedge maple contain milky sap.

- 1403 NE 6th Ave., 7'2" c, 2'3" d
- 1115 SW King St., 8'2" c, 2'7" d

Acer macrophyllum

(*ā*-ser mak-rō-*fill*-um)

Bigleaf maple
Deciduous

Acer macrophyllum, Bigleaf maple. 12954 SW Howell Park Rd., Sauvie Island. 4-28-91. 28' c, 8'11" d. The largest specimen in Greater Portland. The owner will allow motorists to drive around the tree and then exit.

Sometimes considered a weed in the Pacific Northwest, the bigleaf maple can become a massive, beautiful tree. Its potential height is generally less than 100 feet. As the common name implies, its leaves are big—the biggest of all the maples—sometimes attaining over a foot in width. The fall foliage turns yellow, gold, and copper. Frequently this tree grows multiple trunks, usually because it was cut off as a sapling, then produced several potential trunks from the sides of the cut the following year. In early spring, blossom clumps can be quite a spectacle of yellow-green.

The largest bigleaf maple in Oregon is in Jewell, a town in the northern Coast Range, and measured nearly 35 feet in circumference in 1977.

Acer macrophyllum, Bigleaf maple. 3-31-91. The flower.

The Pow-Wow Maple, a relic of Oregon's early days, still stands near the Clackamas River in Gladstone. This ancient tree is on the Rinearson Land Claim of 1846. Clackamas Indians, peaceable and friendly, lived nearby and later were under Rinearson protection. Three Native American chiefs were identified with activities centering around the Pow-Wow Maple: Wacheno, Clackamas Jake, and Clackamas George. An Indian racetrack was adjacent to the maple, and the tree also marked the entrance to the first state fair, which the pioneers held on the Rinearson claim in October 1861.

The present tree is merely a remnant. At one time it was in danger of being removed to widen the road, but it was marked as a historical site in 1937. The Gladstone *Banner-Courier* wrote for the occasion: "With perhaps a half dozen men lynched on it and many Indian pow-wows held under it, the glorious old maple tree . . . has come into public recognition for the first time." It again survived a city council order to remove it in 1967.

- 6733 N Greeley Ave., 21' c, 6'8" d
- NW 11th Dr. & Division St., Gresham, 18'6" c, 5'11" d (planted in the 1800s by Dr. John Powell for whom Powell Blvd. is named)
- corner Monroe & 39th St., Milwaukie, 17'9" c, 5'8" d
- 14170 SW Pacific Hwy., Tigard, 17'4" c, 5'6" d (three trees planted by Wilson M. Tigard, founder of Tigard, in 1861, of which one tree has been struck by lightning)
- 6834 N Villard Ave., 16'6" c, 5'3" d
- 01404 SW Mary Failing Dr., 16'4" c, 5'2" d
- 330 W Powell Blvd., Gresham, 16'c, 5'1" d (saved by the fifth grade class at West Gresham Grade School when Powell Blvd. was widened)
- X 2300 SW Laurel St., 15'10" c, 5' d
- 2126 NE 15th Ave., 15' c, 4'9" d

Acer macrophyllum, Bigleaf maple. 250 Clackamas Blvd., Gladstone. 12-2-89. The Pow-Wow Maple, a relic of the early days, still stands near the Clackamas River in Gladstone.

Acer macrophyllum, Bigleaf maple. 5017 SW Maple Ln. 5-3-91. 16′2″ c, 5′2″ d. The trunk of this very old tree has a large hole in the center.

Acer negundo 'Variegatum', Ghost tree or Variegated box elder. 12175 SW 9th St., Beaverton. 5-16-91. 6' c, 1'11" .d.

Acer negundo 'Variegatum'

(ā-ser ne-*goon*-dō ver-i-*gā*-tum)

Ghost tree or Variegated box elder
Deciduous

The box elder is native to the whole of North America. Sometimes considered a weed, it readily germinates from seed, suckers badly, and harbors the box elder bug. The leaves of this tree do not resemble those of most of the maples in that they have three to five leaflets. Often the terminal leaflet is trilobal. The angle of the twin seeds is very acute, with the wing curved inward. Male and female flowers are always on separate trees. Although short-lived, this box elder is fast-growing and can reach a height of 50 to 75 feet with a wide spread.

The Portland area has many box elders of both the common green and the variegated types.

- 3568 NE Couch St. (two common green trees)
- X 3053 SE Pine St.

Acer palmatum

(ā-ser pall-*mā*-tum)

Japanese maple
Deciduous

Acer palmatum, Japanese maple. 2367 NW Kearney St. 4-16-90. This classic specimen is one of the oldest and biggest in Portland.

The specific name of this tree derives from its resemblance to the palm of a hand with the fingers spread. Originally from China, Korea, and Japan, the Japanese maple is widely grown and hybridized all over the temperate world. Usually a small tree, it never attains much more than 50 feet in height. The varieties now in cultivation present a myriad of colors and leaf shapes (though practically all retain the five to nine lobes) and colors. In the fall this tree in all its variations presents superb colors. Seed wings diverge at an obtuse angle.

Acer palmatum, Japanese maple. 1121 NW 26th Ave. 10-25-90. Actually two trees, both at the height of fall color.

Acer platanoides

(*ā*-ser plat-an-*oy*-dēz)

Norway maple
Deciduous

Acer platanoides 'Harlequin', Norway maple. 4028 SE Salmon St. 10-23-90. 3'2" c, 1' d. The leaves have a white border.

A native to nearly all Europe and into the Near East as far as Iran, this tree is sometimes confused with the planetree or sycamore, though the difference is easy to distinguish: the bark of the Norway maple is very dark and has fine vertical fissures, its reddish petioles emit a milky substance when broken, and it has the typical maple winged seed (these wings spread nearly horizontally). Potentially growing to a height of 90 feet, it more likely tops out at 60 to 70 feet. One dwarf variety ('Almira') only grows to about 16 feet high in 30 years. The Norway maple has many varieties, each emphasizing a different characteristic such as leaf color, size, or shape. It makes a handsome and hardy street tree and is much used for that purpose in the city (e.g., in the median of West Burnside from the river to the North Park Blocks). One of the first maples to bloom in the spring, it can be easily spotted by its bright greenish-yellow small blossom clumps, which might be mistaken for newly emerging leaves.

Acer platanoides, Norway maple. Corner SE 23rd Ave. & Lambert St. 6-18-91. 7'3" c, 2'4" d. A fine, old specimen with green leaves.

Acer pseudoplatanus

(ā-ser soo-dō-*plat*-an-us)

Sycamore maple
Deciduous

Acer pseudoplatanus, Sycamore maple. 1507 SE Salmon St. 7-12-90. 8'9" c, 2'9" d.

As the common name suggests, this tree resembles a sycamore, both in leaf shape and bark habits. Indeed, in England it is called a sycamore. The seeds, however, are typically maplelike, with wings set in a V-formation and hanging in pendulous panicles much like the bigleaf maple. The sycamore maple, a native of mountainous areas in both Europe and western Asia, can attain a height of about 100 feet, making it the most massive of European maple species. Unlike the maple it somewhat resembles—the Norway maple (*A. platanoides*)—this tree does not become colorful in the fall.

- 1535 SW Montgomery Dr. (part of a row of seven trees)

Acer rubrum

(ā-ser rū-brum)

Red maple
Deciduous

Acer rubrum, Red maple. 1130 SW King Ave. 3-26-91. 7'10" c, 2'6" d. Lacy red blossoms on mature trees.

A native of eastern North America with a multitude of varieties, the red maple can grow in very moist ground and is sometimes called "swamp maple." In the wild it reaches 120 feet, while as a city street tree it is a fast grower up to about 40 feet. Its spring flowers, which appear before the leaves, are bright red and attractive, and its fall foliage ranges from orangey-red to scarlet, depending on where it grows and the variety.

- corner SE 7th Ave. & Lambert St., 10' c, 3'2" d

Acer rubrum, Red maple. NE 21st Ave. & Hancock St. 11-4-90. One specimen in a row of red maples that makes quite a statement in the fall. The variety is unknown.

Acer saccharinum, Silver maple. 2105 SE Taylor St. 9-12-90. 16′8″ c. 5′4″ d.

Acer saccharinum

(ā-ser sak-kar-ī-num)

Silver maple
Deciduous

An easy way to identify this maple is to watch it when the wind blows, for the underside of its pointy, five-lobed leaves is silvery-white. A fast-growing tree, it provides good shade. The final height it can attain is about 120 feet, and by then its trunk is enormous. To its disadvantage are its lack of good autumn color and its tendency to fall victim to one or more diseases and insects. It blooms and sets seed, which are red at first, before the leaves appear in the spring. The silver maple is native to eastern North America.

- 1515 SW Clifton St., 16′2″ c, 5′2″ d (planted by William Furnish at his house in 1911)
- 931 N Humboldt St.
- 3520 NE Flanders St., 13′10″ c, 4′5″ d

Acer saccharum

(ā-ser sak-*kar*-um)

Sugar maple
Deciduous

Acer saccharum, Sugar maple. 3715 N Baldwin St. 10-17-90. 9'3" c, 2'11" d. When the roots of this tree pushed up the nearby sidewalk, Portland's Forestry Division and the Bureau of Maintenance joined efforts to save the tree in 1990. They narrowed a new sidewalk, moved a neighbor's fence, and saved all the roots, thus ensuring the tree a healthy, longer life.

The sugar maple is not often found in the West. A native of eastern Canada and the United States, it is one of the most colorful maples in the fall, but it tends to not achieve this display in warmer climates. As the common name implies, this maple is the source of maple sugar. With a sap content of 1–4 percent sucrose, it takes about 30 to 40 gallons of sap to make one gallon of maple syrup. A tree is not tappable until it is at least 35 years old. A slow grower, the tree has a height potential of about 120 feet, but more often attains about 75 feet.

- corner C Ave. & 3rd St., Lake Oswego, 14' c, 4'5" d
- South Park Blocks (15 trees)

Acer saccharum, Sugar maple. Reed College in front of Eliot Hall. 10-23-90. Proof that this species can reach a colorful state in Portland.

Aesculus glabra, Ohio buckeye. Corner SW Main St. & King Ave. 10-12-90. 5'4" c, 1'8"d. One of the few Ohio buckeyes growing on a Portland street.

Aesculus glabra

(*es*-kū-lus *gla*-bra)

Ohio buckeye
Deciduous

Leaf shape shows that this tree is related to the horsechestnuts. It does not reach the huge size of the common horsechestnut, and its blossoms, which are greenish yellow, are not as spectacular, but its fall color more than makes up for these shortcomings. The leaves develop a brilliant orange-red to reddish brown early in the fall. The species acquired its common name because its seeds (also called *nuts*), like those of its relatives the other horsechestnuts, resemble the eyes of a buck.

- 1962 NW Kearney St., 4'8" c, 1'6" d (less than half of original tree)

Aesculus hippocastanum

(*es*-kū-lus hip-ō-kas-*tā*-num)

Common horsechestnut
Deciduous

Aesculus hippocastanum, Common horsechestnut. X 2045 SW 16th Ave. 5-3-91. 18'8" c, 6' d. Planted as a sprouting seed in 1914 by Newton Langerman when he was a boy living in the house to the south.

The horsechestnut, native to mountainous Greece and Albania, is a large tree with large spring blossoms, large leaves, and relatively large nuts. The nuts are a problem in the fall to pedestrians walking on the sidewalks under these trees. Portland will no longer permit this tree to be planted along the streets, although there are two seedless cultivars that are allowed. All horsechestnuts have toxic seeds, flowers, and leaves.

Many, many streets are lined with these mammoths, making a beautiful show in the spring.

- 4011 SE Woodward St., 12'7" c, 4' d
- 1439 SW Columbia St., 9'7" c, 3'1" d
- 1046 SW King St., 11' c, 3'6" d (planted by Amos King around 1870)
- 1216 SE Sellwood Blvd.
- 8206 SE 7th Ave.
- 2211 SW Park Pl.
- 1455 NE Going St.
- 2115 SW Salmon St.
- NE Hancock St. & 15th Ave.
- NE Rodney Ave., between
  Jessup St. & Jarrett St. (allée)

Aesculus hippocastanum, Common horsechestnut. Corner SW Broadway Dr. & Arden Rd. 4-25-90. 11'8" c, 3'9" d. The neighborhood saved this tree from being cut down by a developer.

Aesculus octandra

(*es*-kū-lus ok-*tan*-dra)

Yellow buckeye
Deciduous

Aesculus octandra, Yellow buckeye. 3387 SE Tibbetts St. 5-22-91. 8'4" c, 2'8" d.

This buckeye, considered the most beautiful of them all, can reach 80 feet in height and, when mature, has a nice upright-oval crown. The leaves turn orange in the fall. The bark has varied-colored plates and scales, and the blossoms, although not showy, are panicles of yellow-green flowers about 7 inches high. This tree's seeds, which are smooth and pear-shaped, distinguish it in the fall from the Ohio buckeye. Its native habitat ranges from Pennsylvania to Tennessee and northern Georgia, west to Ohio and Illinois.

- 5511 SE 44th Ave., 8' c, 2'7" d

Aesculus octandra, Yellow buckeye. 5-22-91. The bloom.

Aesculus × *carnea*

(*es*-kū-lus kar-*nē*-a)

Red horsechestnut
Deciduous

The red horsechestnut is a cross between *A. hippocastanum* and *A. pavia*. Smaller than the common horsechestnut, it has the same general shape, making it a fine street tree except for its many big, slightly spiny nuts that drop in the fall. An unusual feature of this hybrid is that, for the most part, it breeds true from the seeds. It is one of the most popular trees in England.

Portland has many beautiful red horsechestnuts. The hue of the blossoms can vary from tree to tree. When several trees are planted in a row, the effect is most attractive.

- X 1725 SW Spring St., 5'10" c, 1'10" d
- 678 NW Melinda
- 1825 SW Elm St.

Aesculus × *carnea,* Red horsechestnut. Between SW 20th Ave. & 20th Pl. on Yamhill St. 4-17-90. 4'11" c, 1'7" d.

Ailanthus altissima

(ā-*lan*-thus al-*tis*-si-ma)

Tree of heaven
Deciduous

This was the tree that grew in Brooklyn, for those of you old enough to remember. The tree of heaven has an amazing ability to grow anywhere, including through concrete. The botanic name means a "tree that can grow up to the sky," and, indeed, this tree can attain a height of 100 feet, with compound leaves providing a nice pattern against the sky. A native of China, this tree was introduced to Europe in 1751 and to the United States in 1784. Many horticulturists find no redeeming feature in it, but since it is truly a city tree, it can provide greenery where nothing else will grow. The males and females are separate trees; the male flower has a disagreeable odor and the female seeds rattle in the wind throughout the winter.

The Portland area has many trees of heaven of all shapes and sizes.

- 2101 SW Yamhill St.
- 700 NW Marlborough Ave., 8'10" c, 2'10" d
- 1505 SE Taylor St., 8'5" c, 2'8" d

Ailanthus altissima, Tree of heaven. 4524 SE 41st Ave. 7-27-90.

Albizia julibrissin

(al-*biz*-i-a jū-li-*bri*-sin)

Silk tree
Deciduous

When the silk tree blooms in late summer, it gives an exotic, tropical impression. The profuse, dark, pinky-red flowers, coming at a time when most trees have finished blooming, resemble small, fluffy brushes. Even the leaves, which are compound, look semi-tropical and at night they droop and close up. Consequently, the name of the tree in Japan means "sleepy tree." Native from Iran to central China, it was introduced into cultivation in the United States in 1745. When Portland has a hard winter, the tree can have difficulty. This plus a vascular wilt disease to which it is susceptible, make having a healthy silk tree somewhat chancy, though Portland has a number of them. If it gets the sun and warmth it needs, the tree will achieve an umbrella shape and a height of about 60 feet.

- 7855 SE 16th Ave.
- X 2161 SW Yamhill St., 4'9" c, 1'6" d
- 3731 E Burnside St.
- 2136 SW Vista Ave.

Albizia julibrissin, Silk tree. SE 17th Ave. & Ellis St. 7- 27-90. 6'11" c, 2'2" d.

Araucaria araucana

(a-ra-*kar*-i-a a-ra-*kā*-na)

Monkey puzzle
Evergreen

Araucaria araucana, Monkey puzzle. 2411 SE Tamarack Ave. 10-23-90. 5'3" c, 1'8" d. More than half the monkey puzzles in Portland are larger than this male.

Originally from Chile, this tree made its way to the Northern Hemisphere via the physician-explorer Archibald Menzies, who, at the end of the 18th century, took seeds with him, germinated them on shipboard, and arrived in England with small trees. Many of Portland's 150 monkey puzzles were planted in the early 1900s, having arrived as seeds brought by sailors or having been passed out as tiny trees from the South American display at Portland's Lewis & Clark Exposition in 1905. Botanists consider the species to be the most primitive living conifer, with fossils dating back 70 million years.

Monkey puzzles are hardy trees, surviving wind and ice intact. They are easy to spot, especially in the winter, because of their unusual limb shape and rounded crown. Males and females are separate trees. The largest monkey puzzles in Oregon are two in the Astoria area that measure 9'6" in circumference.

- NE Hazelfern Pl. & Flanders St.
- 3406 SE Gladstone St.
- 4133 SE Belmont St.
- 9620 N Central St.

Arbutus menziesii

(ar-*bū*-tus men-*zē*-sē-ī)

Pacific madrone or Madrona
Evergreen

Arbutus menziesii, Pacific madrone or Madrona. 601 1st St., Lake Oswego. 4-29-90. 8'9" c, 2'9" d.

This native broadleaf evergreen sheds its leaves and bark bit by bit, making it a rather messy tree for a garden. It compensates, however, with elegance, especially in the early spring when it blooms profusely and in the fall when it is covered with fruit (much liked by the birds). Throughout the year its trunk is a beautiful color and texture, particularly on the older specimens. A tree capable of growing in many types of soil, it seems to like bluffs, frequently shooting out at an angle from the side of a bluff. In favorable conditions it can attain 100 feet in height and 4 feet in diameter. Dr. Archibald Menzies, who accompanied Captain George Vancouver in exploring the West Coast, discovered the species in 1792 on the Olympic Peninsula.

Bess Kaiser Hospital stands on a bluff that at one time was called Madrona Hill. Before any buildings were constructed on this bluff overlooking Swan Island, it was covered with madronas. Today only a few trees remain standing. A drive to the end of N Emerson St. will provide a view of the madronas still there, although a fire in August 1991 may have destroyed many of these trees. Imagine what the bluff looked like 50 years ago!

- SW Capitol Highway & Nevada Ct., 10' c, 3'2" d
- 1125 NE 242nd Ave., Gresham, 9'4" c, 3' d
- N Willamette Blvd., Wabash Ave. & Bryant St., 7'3" c, 2'4" d
- X 2525 N Sumner St., 9'4" c, 3' d
- N Greeley Ave. & Humboldt St.

Arbutus menziesii, Pacific madrone or Madrona. 2435 N Wygant St. 4-11-91. 9'7" c, 3'1" d

Arbutus menziesii, Pacific madrone or Madrona. 6114 NE Willow St. 8-11-91. 8'6" c, 2'8" d. The lovely peeling bark is typical of this tree. The new bark is butter smooth and pale, pale green.

Betula nigra

(*bet*-ū-la *nī*-gra)

River birch
Deciduous

Betula nigra, River birch. SE 7th Ave. & Malden, Sellwood Park. 7-11-91. 9′5″ c, 3′ d. Sellwood Park's big, old river birch.

The bark of a mature river birch has little resemblance to that of the "classic" birch; it is nearly black and deeply vertically fissured. The leaves are not very birchlike either; they are irregularly oval, glossy dark green above and whitish underneath. Native to the eastern half of the United States, it is the only native birch at low elevations in the Southeast, where it prefers stream banks, ponds, and swamps. The multitrunked form is typical of this fast grower, which reaches an ultimate height of 90 feet.

Sellwood has two river birches, one particularly large and quite old. The other, younger one still has some birchlike bark visible on the upper limbs.

- 710 SE Lambert St., 8′11″ c, 2′10″ d

Betula papyrifera, Paper birch. Corner SE Stark St. & 52nd Ave. 4-2-91. 8'6" c, 2'8" d.

Betula papyrifera

(*bet*-ū-la pap-i-*rif*-er-a)

Paper birch
Deciduous

Although the paper birch is native to Oregon, its natural habitat is in the northeast corner of the state. Its entire habitat stretches from Labrador to British Columbia as far south as Oregon, Nebraska, and Pennsylvania. Unlike the European white birch, this birch's bark peels easily and has been used for canoes and wigwam covers. Capable of reaching 120 feet in height, the tree is usually smaller than that at maturity. Its limbs are much less susceptible to ice storms than are those of the European white birch.

- 6304 N Burrage Ave., 7'9" c, 2'6" d
- 1436 SE Taylor St.
- SE Milwaukie Ave. & Haig St., Brooklyn Park (three trees)

Betula pendula

(*bet*-ū-la *pen*-dū-la)

European white birch
Deciduous

Betula pendula 'Dalecarlica', European white birch. 108 NE Laurelhurst Pl. 4-22-91. 11'5" c, 3'8" d. The girth of this cultivar is enormous for the species in Portland.

This birch is sometimes difficult to distinguish from its North American cousin, the paper birch. As one might guess from the specific name, the European birch tends to have more pendulous branches. Also, its bark does not peel so readily; instead, it becomes quite riddled with black splotches as it ages. Over time, this medium- to fast-growing tree can reach 100 feet in height, with a spread one-half to two-thirds the height. Native to Europe and Asia Minor, it grows up to the 6500-foot level in the Pyrenees. Some of Portland's winters—those with a prolonged silver thaw—are devastating to these birches, often leaving them minus huge limbs which must be pruned off after cracking and splitting from the heavy ice. The limbs will regenerate, but the tree loses much of its beauty.

- 8133 SE 7th Ave., 9' c, 2'10" d

Betula pendula 'Dalecarlica', a popular cultivar of this birch, has deeply lobed leaves.

- 3115 NW Thurman St., 12'4" c, 3'11" d (measured at ground level because of multiple trunks)
- 2807 NE 18th Ave., 10' c, 3'2" d
- 7152 SE 13th Ave., 9'5" c, 3' d
- 7140 SE Reed College Pl., 9' c, 2'10" d
- 6428 SE Reed College Pl., 8'11" c, 2'10" d
- 904 SE Lambert St., 8'9" c, 2'9" d

Calocedrus decurrens, Incense cedar. 8602 N Woolsey Ave. 3-15-90. 7' c, 2'3" d. Perfect examples of the columnar form. The house was built in 1906; perhaps the trees were planted shortly thereafter.

Calocedrus decurrens

(kal-ō-*sēd*-rus dē-*ker*-enz)

Incense cedar
Evergreen

A native of southern Oregon, spots near Mount Hood and Bend, and montane California, this tree is most often seen in its columnar form when growing as an ornamental in the city. Several specimens are frequently planted together for screens and hedges. Distinguishing it among the cedarlike conifers can be very difficult, if not impossible, from a car. Two features identify the incense cedar—if one can see the tree up close: the free tips of adjacent scale leaves are equal in length, thus appearing as groups of four at the node, and the cones are elongate, up to an inch long, and look like litle urns until they open up to resemble duck bills. The incense cedar has about a 500-year life span. Its name refers to the pleasant odor of the foliage and the wood.

- 1144 SE 55th Ave., 11' c, 3'6" d (Quimby house built in 1904, but the tree may predate the house)
- 3022 N Ainsworth St., 10'6" c, 3'4" d
- 4849 N Girard St.
- 662 7th St., Lake Oswego

Carpinus betulus

(kar-*pī*-nus *bet*-ū-lus)

European hornbeam
Deciduous

Carpinus betulus, European hornbeam. In Oaks Park, at the end of Oaks Park Way between Area 12 & Area 15 & the Willamette River. 6-18-91. 12'5" c, 3'11" d. One of three fully mature, outstanding examples of the species.

Much used in Europe for roadside planting and hedges, this tree is native to Europe from southeast England to the Caucasus. It can reach a height of over 100 feet but more likely grows to 40 to 60 feet, with a spread of 30 to 40 feet, making it a fine small landscape tree. It has a dense, oval crown and smooth bark much like the European beech. Male (small and thin) and female (larger) flowers, in the form of green catkins, are borne on the same tree, the female catkin becoming an attractive, multiseeded, pendulous cluster in June. Portland has few large hornbeams, a pity because they are so attractive. Small cultivars of this tree are growing in several spots about town and can be identified in June when they produce their (sometimes sparse) seed clusters.

Carpinus betulus, European hornbeam. 6-18-91. A seed cluster.

Carpinus caroliniana

(kar-*pī*-nus ka-rō-lin-i-*ā*-na)

American hornbeam
Deciduous

Carpinus caroliniana, American hornbeam. 4327 SE Ellis St. 6-27-91. 5'10" c, 1'10" d.

A slow growing, attractive tree never more than 40 feet tall, the American hornbeam fits well in a parking strip. It generally has a wide-spreading, flat top. The green catkin flowers, with both males and females on the same tree, turn into seed-bearing, drooping bracts that make it easy to distinguish this species. The blue-gray bark on older trees is smooth with sinews. For a tree that likes moist soil, it is surprising that this hornbeam, native to the entire United States east of the Mississippi, is extremely rare in Portland.

- 2218 NE 9th Ave., 3'5" c, 1'1" d (two trees)

Carpinus caroliniana, American hornbeam. 6-27-91. A seed cluster.

Carya ovata

(*ke*-ri-a ō-*vā*-ta)

Shagbark hickory
Deciduous

Carya ovata, Shagbark hickory. X 3556 SE Gladstone St. 8-27-90. 6′ c, 1′11″ d. These young but handsome trees have been pollarded; therefore, their shape is not typical of the species.

Native from Quebec to Minnesota, south to Georgia and Texas, the shagbark hickory can grow to 120 feet. Its leaves are alternate and pinnately compound, always with five leaflets. The tree gets its name from the shaggy bark that develops as it ages, consisting of thin plates, loose at both ends. The nuts of this tree are edible, and the wood produces the renowned hickory smoke for hams and bacon. This hickory is a handsome tree, rare in Portland, with a straight trunk and cylindrical crown.

- SW 2nd Ave. & Woods St., front of Children's Museum, 5′7″ c, 1′9″ d

Carya tomentosa

(*ke*-ri-a tō-men-*tō*-sa)

Mockernut hickory
Deciduous

Carya tomentosa, Mockernut hickory. X 8223 SE 16th Ave. 9-25-90. 7'7" c, 2'5" d. This old tree stands beside a house that was built in the 1890s; perhaps the first owner brought the mockernuts from the East.

This hickory has fragrant, compound leaves. The nut is thick-walled and enclosed in the four-grooved husk that splits nearly completely open when ripe. Even so, the kernel is difficult to extract. Like the shagbark hickory, this hickory's native habitat is almost all the United States east of the Mississippi. When mature, its height can be 80 feet.

Castanea dentata, American chestnut. Corner SE 11th Ave. & Lexington St. 5-22-91. 14'6" c, 4'7" d. Two American chestnuts, perhaps the only two in Greater Portland, growing very close together.

Castanea dentata

(kas-*tā*-nē-a den-*tāt*-a)

American chestnut
Deciduous

Once native and common from Maine to Mississippi, starting in 1904 the American chestnut has been nearly decimated by a blight, *Endothia parasitica,* that entered this country on either Chinese or Japanese seedling chestnuts in the late 1800s. Very few trees now remain, especially in the East. Truly a magnificent tree in stature, it is capable of reaching 120 feet in height and 13 to 17 feet in diameter. It does not have the spreading habit of its European cousin *Castanea sativa.* In the 1800s it was an important lumber tree in the eastern United States because the wood is resistant to decay, making it made prime fencing material and telegraph poles.

While many trees are identified in Greater Portland as American chestnuts, careful inspection proves them to be either the European or the Chinese chestnut instead.

Castanea sativa

(kas-*tā*-nē-a sa-*tī*-va)

Spanish or European chestnut
Deciduous

Castanea sativa, Spanish or European chestnut. 4619 N Michigan Ave. 8-23-90. 15'9" c, 5' d. Planted in 1891 by June McMillan Ordway at the then-new Patton Home.

A mature tree of this species certainly clarifies the words "under the spreading chestnut tree," although, in fact, the tree that inspired Longfellow was actually a common horsechestnut (*Aesculus hippocastanum*). With a wide and rounded crown, a mature tree can reach heights of over 100 feet and an age of over 1000 years. Most attractive in July and August when the yellow male catkins and light yellow forming nuts are prominent, it needs to be cross-pollinated, and a solitary tree with none nearby will produce few nuts. Like its American cousin *Castanea dentata*, the European chestnut is susceptible to the chestnut blight, but to a lesser degree.

- 1770 SW Prospect Dr., 16' c, 5'1" d (planted in 1923 by Max Hirsch)
- 2401 SE 26th Ave. (planted in 1883 by the family of Vivian Bretherton)
- 114 SW Kingston Ave.
- 1628 NE Thompson St.
- SE Stark St. between 49th & 50th Aves. (several trees)

Castanea sativa, Spanish or European chestnut. 2853 NE 56th Ave. 7-27-90. 14'8" c, 4'8" d. Freda Frauendorf planted this tree in 1912 before the streets were paved. Her husband made her plant it on the street corner because he said she had enough trees in the yard. It is called "Freda's tree."

Catalpa bignonioides

(ka-*tal*-pa big-nō-ni-*oy*-dēz)

Southern catalpa
Deciduous

Catalpa bignonioides, Southern catalpa. 7-12-91. The bloom.

The name of this tree comes from a Creek Indian word—*kutuhlpa*—and its native habitat is Florida, Georgia, Louisiana, and Mississippi. Although it can grow to a height of 65 feet, it generally only attains about 35 feet, with an equal or greater spread. The leaves are long-stalked, huge (up to 8 inches long and wide), and slightly hairy underneath, especially on the veins. They tend to have an unpleasant odor when crushed (the leaves of the northern catalpa do not have this quality). The flowers of this tree and the northern catalpa are very similar, both being clusters of bell-shaped blooms, white with yellow and purple spots. The clusters of this tree tend to be about 4 inches longer than those of the northern catalpa, however, making quite a show in late June to early July (usually about two weeks later than those of its northern counterpart). The seed pods that follow and remain on the tree all winter are long (up to 20 inches) and very skinny.

- 4033 SE Woodstock Blvd. 8'4" c,
  2'8" d (four trees)
- 5533 N Maryland St. 10'6" c, 3'4" d

Catalpa bignonioides, Southern catalpa. SE 26th Ave. & Main St. 9-12-90. 9' c, 2'10" d. The long seed pods.

Catalpa speciosa

(ka-*tal*-pa spē-si-ō-sa)

Northern catalpa
Deciduous

Catalpa speciosa, Northern catalpa. NW 28th Ave. & Upshur St. 6-27-91. 8'10" c, 2'10" d. One of four large catalpas in a row.

With enormous leaves and beautiful late spring or early summer flowers, this catalpa is native from southern Illinois and Indiana to western Tennessee and northern Arkansas. Even in the winter when all the leaves have left, the tree can be spotted by its pendulous, skinny seed pods that can reach 23 inches in length. In the wild this catalpa reaches 150 feet in height, but in the city it is usually about 40 feet high, with almost as wide a spread. The bark is deeply furrowed and dark, and the wood is extremely resistant to rot. Early trees were planted by pioneers to provide axe and shovel handles until they found that Oregon white oak better served their purposes.

- 2816 NE 9th Ave., 13' c, 4'2" d (two trees)
- 2826 NE 24th Ave., 10'9" c, 3'5" d (two trees)
- SE Lafayette St. & 26th Ave., Powell Park, 8'7" c, 2'9" d
- SE Powell Blvd. & 26th Ave.
- 5306 SE 37th Ave.

Catalpa speciosa, Northern catalpa. 6-27-91. The bloom.

Cedrus atlantica
Cedrus deodara
Cedrus libani

(*sē*-drus at-*lan*-ti-ka)
(dē-ō-*dar*-a)
(*lib*-an-ī)

Atlas cedar
Deodar
Cedar of Lebanon
Evergreen

Cedrus atlantica 'Glauca', Blue atlas cedar. X 2005 NE
17th Ave. 3-30-91. 12' c, 3'10" d.

We have grouped these three cedar species together because it is often difficult to distinguish one from the other, especially when they are big, tall, and old. Some botanists regard them as geographical forms of one species. In any case, they are at least very closely related. A local arborist distinguishes the three on the basis of their limbs: those of the atlas go up at the ends, those of the Lebanon go out straight, and those of the deodar go down and droop at the ends. The cones are difficult to look at closely because they are generally high in the tree and they usually disintegrate on the tree after two years. The native habitats are distinct at this time, although in ancient geological times the three formed a more-or-less continuous forest: atlases come from Algeria and Morocco, deodars from the Himalayas, and Lebanons from Asia Minor—Lebanon to Turkey. Their closest relative—and it's not very close—is the larch.

The most common form of the atlas in this area is the blue atlas, where the foliage is definitely gray-blue. Deodar foliage tends to be a light gray-green, and Lebanon foliage a dark or bright green. While Portland has many true cedars that are easy to spot, one place offers all three species, including the two forms of the atlas cedar: on the Eastmoreland Golf Course, directly across from 6438 SE 28th Ave. (from left to right they are Lebanon, green atlas, blue atlas, and, behind the hedge, deodar).

Cedrus atlantica
- 1609 SE 16th Ave., 11'2" c, 3'7" d
- 3935 SW Corbett Ave.
- X 2325 N Sumner St., 13' c, 4'2" d
- X 2005 NE 17th Ave., 12' c, 3'10" d

Cedrus atlantica 'Glauca', Blue atlas cedar. 8-15-91. New male cones on a branch.

Cedrus deodara, Deodar. 8421 SW Macadam Rd. 3-22-91. 11'7" c, 3'8" d. Planted about 1890.

Cedrus libani, Cedar of Lebanon. 1425 SW 20th Ave. 2-16-91. 13'8" c, 4'4" d. Planted about 1870 by Henry Miller, an early nursery owner.

Cedrus deodara
- SW Wright, Park, & Rose Garden Blvd., 11'c, 3'6" d
- 5019 SE Stark St.

Cedrus libani
- Church St. & Furnace St., Lake Oswego, 11'10" c, 3'9" d (two trees)
- 6441 NE Oregon, 11'3" c, 3'7" d
- West A St. & McKillican St., West Linn, 11' c, 3'6" d
- 3407 SW Brentwood Dr., 10' c, 3'2" d

Cercidiphyllum japonicum, Katsura tree. 1132 SW Vista Ave. 5-9-91. 8'5" c, 2'8" d. A 50-year-old tree.

Cercidiphyllum japonicum

(ser-si-di-*fīl*-um ja-*pon*-i-kum)

Katsura tree
Deciduous

The specific name signifies that this tree is native to Japan. Introduced to the nursery trade in 1865, this generally multitrunked tree can attain a height of around 80 feet. Male and female flowers are on separate trees. The leaves are attractive—heart-shaped with red stalks—and they turn a lovely yellow to orange in the fall. As a slow-growing tree, the katsura easily fits into a smaller garden for many years. It is not a common tree in the Portland area.

- 1927 SW Jefferson St.
- 2161 SW Laurel St. (two trees)
- Oregon Art Institute Sculpture Court, SW 10th Ave. across from the YWCA (row of nine trees)
- SW Park Ave. between Columbia & Clay Sts. (row of 10 trees)

Cercis canadensis, Eastern redbud. 21595 NW Sauvie Island Rd., Sauvie Island. 4-28-91. A rare tree in Portland, the height and shape of this specimen, the largest in the area, are typical of the species.

Cercis canadensis

(*ser*-sis kan-a-*den*-sis)

Eastern redbud
Deciduous

This relatively small tree is an early bloomer, the striking dark pink blossoms appearing before the leaves are out and lasting 2 to 3 weeks. Oklahoma's state tree, it is a native of the eastern United States from the mid-Atlantic states to northern Florida. It has been called "a native tree with a touch of class." Its top height is never much beyond 30 feet, while a California cousin, the Western redbud, is still smaller.

- 2905 SE Harrison St., Milwaukie
- corner 162nd Ave. & Burnside St. (three trees)
- NT 3924 SE 33rd Pl., 3'9" c, 1'2" d (two trees)

Chamaecyparis lawsoniana

(kam-e-*sip*-a-ris law-sō-ni-*ā*-na)

Port Orford cedar
Evergreen

Chamaecyparis lawsoniana, Port Orford cedar. SE 31st Ave. & Tibbetts St. 9-25-90. An exceedingly handsome variety of this species.

Not a cedar at all, this member of the cypress family is sometimes confused with the Western redcedar, but its branches have a more delicate, almost feathery appearance. A look at the underside of the branchlets will identify it: it will have small silver X's at the intersections of the flattened leaves. The small, round cones also are diagnostic. Bluish or whitish when young, they turn red-brown after a year when they mature. Each scale of the cone has a small, curved point in the center. There are over 200 forms of this species, some having yellow or blue foliage rather than the usual green. Some forms are spreading, others are columnar. The Port Orford cedar is susceptible to a root rot—a soil-borne fungal disease that kills the tree and for which there is no known cure. The largest Port Orford cedar in Oregon measured over 37 feet in circumference and 219 feet in height in 1968. It is still alive.

- 879 NE Ainsworth St., 12′ c, 3′10″ d
- NE Holliday St. between 6th & 7th Aves., 10′2″ c, 3′3″ d
- 1627 NE Thompson St. (a blue form), 8′6″ c, 2′8″ d
- 5327 NE Cleveland Ave.
- 830 SE Sellwood Blvd. (a yellow form)
- corner SW 4th Ave. & Jefferson St. (two trees, one felled by the Columbus Day storm of 1962 and uprighted by Bill Robinson)

Chamaecyparis lawsoniana, Port Orford cedar. SE 26th Ave., Lone Fir Cemetery. 9-13-90. An attractive long row bordering the street.

Chamaecyparis lawsoniana, Port Orford cedar. 5-16-91. New cones.

Chamaecyparis nootkatensis

(kam-e-*sip*-a-ris noot-ka-*ten*-sis)

Alaska cedar
Evergreen

Chamaecyparis nootkatensis, Alaska cedar. SW Fischer Ln., Hoyt Arboretum (near Bristlecone Pine Trail). 6-26-91. A row of mature trees planted in 1963.

The Alaska cedar has a wilted appearance. Compared to the Port Orford cedar, the branchlets of this cedar have a rougher texture than those of the Port Orford cedar and are lacking the silver X's on the underside, while the cones are longer and take two seasons to mature rather than one. A native from coastal Alaska to the Cascades in Oregon, this tree is prized for its yellow wood used for interior finish. Its ultimate height can be more than 175 feet and its lifespan can be 3500 years.

- 5732 SE Yamhill St.
- 3283 SE Gilham Ave. (a grove)

Cladrastis lutea

(kla-*dras*-tis lū-*tē*-a)

Yellowwood
Deciduous

Cladrastis lutea, Yellowwood. SE 28th Ave. at end of Woodstock, East-moreland Golf Course. 5-21-90. 9'2" c, 2'11" d. The largest in a row of five yellowwoods.

A native from North Carolina to Kentucky, Tennessee, and southern Indiana, it is an uncommon tree, although it was introduced to the nursery trade in 1812. The yellowwood has attractive, alternate-pinnately compound leaves and in mid-spring bears many white, fragrant, pendant flower panicles. It is, however, an unreliable bloomer and there may be years where there is little, if any, bloom. At maturity its height can be up to 60 feet, and it has nearly that much spread. Since it is a member of the pea family, its roots support nitrogen-fixing bacteria, which are beneficial for what grows nearby. Many feel this tree is not used nearly enough as an ornamental; Portland has few of these trees.

- NT 5535 SE Madison St., 12'11" c, 4'1" d

Cladrastis lutea, Yellowwood. N Kerby Ave., Peninsula Park. 5-20-90. A small tree in full bloom.

Clerodendrum trichotomum, Glory bower or Harlequin. 5622 N Atlantic Ave. 7-27-90.

Clerodendrum trichotomum

(kler-ō-*den*-drum trī-kō-*tō*-mum)

Glory bower or Harlequin
Deciduous

This very small tree is native to Japan. The leaves, when crushed, smell like peanut butter. Its blossoms, which occur in late summer, are fragrant clusters, white and tubular, and they emerge from scarlet calyces, which stay in place when the seed forms. These blossoms are highly attractive to butterflies; Red Admirals can literally swarm the tree. The seed is a bright metallic blue. New tree starts form from underground roots and have a habit of appearing here and there in the garden, not necessarily where they are wanted.

- 4023 SE Schiller St.

Clerodendrum trichotomum, Glory bower or Harlequin. 10-13-90. Seeds.

Cornus florida

(kōr-nus flōr-i-da)

Flowering or Eastern dogwood
Deciduous

Cornus florida, Flowering or Eastern dogwood. SE 39th Ave. & Taggart St. 4-22-91. Rebecca Kendall, the first owner of the house in the background, brought this tree from Paris and planted it in 1882.

The specific name implies what this tree does to profusion: flower. The flowers (actually large bracts) hide the small leaves as they come out, making the tree appear leafless until the bracts fall off. This tree is also attractive in the fall with its red leaves and bright scarlet fruit. Since the ultimate height seldom exceeds 50 feet, this dogwood is suitable for a front or side yard.

Greater Portland has many eastern dogwoods, both the pink-flowered and white-flowered forms. The pink trees vary from pale to nearly red.

- 2435 N Webster St. (pink)
- 2123 N Emerson St. (white)
- 4107 NE 22nd Ave. (white)

Cornus florida, Flowering or Eastern dogwood. NE 9th Ave. & Mult-nomah St. (in front of Nordstrom). 4-25-91. Originally planted on NE 7th & Holladay in 1882 by Judge Charles Bellinger, this tree was transplanted to its present location in 1956 because of construction of the Lloyd Center.

Cornus nuttallii

(*kōr*-nus nut-*tal*-ē-ī)

Pacific or Western dogwood
Deciduous

Cornus nuttallii, Pacific or Western dogwood. 2944 SE Taylor St. 4-9- 90. 12'10" c, 4'1" d. Portland's largest Pacific dogwood.

Pacific dogwood, as its name implies, is native from southern British Columbia to southern California. It has been called the queen of the West's native hardwoods because of its spectacular spring bloom. What looks like flower petals are actually four to seven white bracts, each up to 3 inches long; the real flowers are multiple and tiny in the center. Sometimes this tree blooms twice a year, once in early spring and once in late summer. If it blooms only once, tiny "flowers," just waiting to enlarge the following spring, are visible over the winter. The tree is also attractive in the fall because of its fruit and red leaves. Look quickly, however, for the birds are very fond of the tight clusters of orange-red, fleshy berries. Unfortunately the Pacific Northwest is losing many of these trees because of a fungal infection called anthracnose.

North Portland seems to have an abundance of Pacific dogwoods, many being a size that suggests old growth where house construction allowed them to remain. Many have reached their full height of 60 feet, suggesting they are well over 100 years old. The largest Pacific dogwood in the state measured 14 feet in circumference and 60 feet in height in 1986.

We are sorry to report that the largest Pacific dogwood we found in Portland (13'8" circumference) was cut down shortly after we measured it.

- corner SE 16th Ave. & Bybee Blvd., 7'7" c, 2'5" d
- 8044 N Richmond Ave., 6'9" c, 2'2" d
- 9 NE Ainsworth St., 7'3" c, 2'4" d
- 5735 NE 29th Ave.
- 5442 SE Milwaukie Ave.
- 6207 SE 46th Ave., 7'10" c, 2'6" d

Cornus nuttallii, Pacific or Western dogwood. Corner N Girard St. & Haven Ave. 4-17-90. A spectacular intersection in April!

Cornus nuttallii, Pacific or Western dogwood. 7510 N Charleston Ave. 4-17-90. A beautiful, big tree with seven trunks.

Crataegus laevigata

(kra-*tē*-gus lē-vi-*gā*-ta)

English hawthorn
Deciduous

Crataegus laevigata, English hawthorn. Corner SW Mitchell St. & Dosch Rd. 4-29-91. 7'7" c, 2'5" d. A large, classic beauty.

Also known as the "May Tree" in England, this species produces the May flowers mentioned in English literature. Its many cultivars offer a great diversity: some have red flowers, others have white; some have double flowers, others have single. Long cultivated, the native habitat of this tree is Europe and northern Africa.

In April the Portland area is full of blooming English hawthorns of all sizes and colors. The small red fruits, which resemble tiny crabapples, remain on the tree through the winter or until the birds consume them.

Crataegus × lavallei

(kra-*tē*-gus la-*val*-ē-ī)

Lavalle or Carriere hawthorn
Deciduous

Crataegus × lavallei, Lavalle hawthorn. 2023 SW Montgomery Dr. 5-20-90.

Although no one is sure of one of this tree's parents, its birth occurred about 1880. The hybridizing seems to have been done by several nursery people about the same time, one of them being a man named Carriere, who described his tree in 1883. The correct name is Lavalle hawthorn; it is sometimes (mistakenly) called the Carriere hawthorn. It is an exceptionally handsome small tree that produces pretty white flowers in the spring and large (up to 0.75 inch in diameter) red pomelike fruit in the fall. The fruit hanging against the lustrous dark green leaves is something to behold and lasts well into early winter. Although 40 feet is its ultimate height, the tree is a slow grower and makes an excellent street tree. Its ultimate crown spread is about 25 feet.

- 2624 NW Cornell Rd., 7'10" c, 2'6" d (three trees)
- 3182 SE Lake Rd., Milwaukie, 7'6" c, 2'5" d

Crataegus × lavallei, Lavalle hawthorn. 3025 SE Crystal Springs Blvd. 11-20-89. 9'2" c, 2'11" d.

Crataegus × lavallei, Lavalle hawthorn. 10-25-90. Fruit.

Cryptomeria japonica

(krip-tō-*me*-ri-a ja-*pon*-i-ka)

Cryptomeria or Japanese cedar
Evergreen

Cryptomeria japonica, Cryptomeria or Japanese cedar. 1005 5th St., Oregon City. 12-2-89. 9'9" c, 3'1" d. The largest cryptomeria in the Portland area.

The cryptomeria is one of Japan's most important timber trees. In its native habitat it can attain over 200 feet. An entire forest of them is most impressive; the trunks, with their reddish-brown, shreddy bark, are very long and straight, like giant telephone poles. The tree has two types of foliage: the juvenile leaves are soft and nearly an inch long, and the mature leaves are shorter and firmer. All the leaves are arranged spirally on the branch. In the winter the foliage can turn reddish brown, suggesting that the tree has died, but the green returns in the spring. The Japanese make huge balls of green cryptomeria branches when they start the new sake batch for the year. The time the branches turn brown coincides with the time the sake has aged enough to drink. The cryptomeria was introduced into the U.S. nursery trade in 1861, but it is an uncommon tree in the Portland area.

- 771 E St., Lake Oswego, 8'10" c, 2'10" d
- 3283 SE Gilham Ave.

Cryptomeria japonica, Cryptomeria or Japanese cedar. 5-4-91. Cones.

Cunninghamia lanceolata

(kun-ing-*ham*-i-a lan-sē-ō-*lā*-ta)

China fir
Evergreen

Cunninghamia lanceolata, China fir. 4339 SE 35th Ave. 9-25-90. This large specimen has six trunks and is impossible to measure.

When people first see this tree, they may wonder if it is sick, but chances are it is not—the needles persist on the branches for around 5 years then die in batches and remain (dry and dead) for several more years. The tree, therefore, has an interesting but rather scruffy appearance. Highly prized in its native China for the easily worked, fragrant, durable wood, it can grow to 150 feet in height in the wild. Unlike most conifers, it has the ability to produce sprouts from the remaining roots after the tree has been cut down. Quite often it is multitrunked.

Although the tree was introduced to the U.S. nursery trade in 1804, the small size of Portland's trees suggests that local nurseries carried this species only fairly recently.

- NT 2750 SW Talbot Rd.
- 580 SW 1st St., Lake Oswego
- 3165 SW 82nd Ave. (three trunks)
- 1104 SE Mall St.
- 14041 E Burnside St.

Cunninghamia lanceolata, China fir. 4-10-91. Cones.

Davidia involucrata, Dove tree or Handkerchief tree. X 1815 SW Montgomery Dr. (look down over the hill). 4-16-90.

Davidia involucrata

(da-*vid*-i-a in-vol-ū-*krā*-ta)

Dove or Handkerchief tree
Deciduous

Grown mostly for its unusual flower head, the dove tree can be temperamental and slow growing, reaching an ultimate height of about 60 feet. It does not bloom until it is 15 to 20 years old, and even after that it may be uncooperative, showing alternate-year patterns at best. The common names come from the flowers and their bracts. The two white bracts are unequal in size; the lower one can be up to 7 inches long and 4 inches wide and the upper bract can be up to 4 inches long and 2 inches wide. They remain on the tree for around two weeks, from mid-April to the first week in May, as a rule. It was the plant explorer, Ernest Henry Wilson, who, on his first expedition to China in 1899, said the tree blooms reminded him of white doves perching and fluttering in the branches. The fruit, which resembles the fruit of a sycamore, hangs on its long stalk until early spring, while the bark is orange, brown, scaly, and handsome in the winter. Native to China, the tree was introduced to the United States in 1904, seven years after the seed arrived in France from China.

Greater Portland has few dove trees. Many of the trees around Oregon are descended from the state's first specimen at the Bush garden in Salem, planted in the early part of this century.

- 2578 SW Montgomery Dr.
- 210 SE 93rd Ave.

Davidia involucrata, Dove tree or Handkerchief tree. 4-18-90. Flowerheads.

Diospyros kaki, Japanese persimmon. 1423 SE Marion St. 11-13-90. One of the very few Japanese persimmons in Portland. The fruit remains on the tree well into November.

Diospyros kaki

(dī-*os*-pir-os *ka*-kē)

Japanese persimmon
Deciduous

A member of the ebony family, this tree has heavy, hard, dark wood that is used for such things as golf club heads and flooring. The best thing about the tree is its fruit, which is about the size of an apple, bright orange and smooth, with orange flesh that is positively delicious when soft and completely ripe. Picked in November, the fruit takes several weeks to become edible. Males and females are on separate trees. A solitary female tree will bear seedless fruit. The foliage of this tree is leathery and handsome, dark green and glossy on the upper side. The tree's potential height is 60 feet, and, as the common name implies, this species is native to Japan. The United States also has a species of persimmon (*Diospyros virginiana*) with smaller fruit much prized by opossums, racoons, and robins. The American persimmon exists in Portland but far from the streets.

The Portland area used to have more Japanese persimmons but they have been cut down in the last 20 years. The local winter is sometimes just a little too cold for these trees.

Eriobotrya japonica

(er-i-ō-*bot*-ri-a ja-*pon*-i-ka)

Loquat
Evergreen

Eriobotrya japonica, Loquat. 2622 SE 12th Ave. 5-8-91. Perhaps the sole loquat on Portland's streets, this tree was grown from seed in the early 1950s by Bishop Daiyu Y. Henjoji.

A beautiful, small, broadleaf evergreen tree, more often found in the South than the North, the loquat originally came from China and Japan and was introduced to the United States in 1784. It has fragrant white flower clusters in the winter, usually from November through January, that produce edible fruit when Portland's winters are on the mild side. A member of the rose family, it rarely exceeds 35 feet in height. According to a Japanese saying, this tree will only bear fruit after the planter has died; in other words, it takes many years for the tree to start blooming.

Fagus sylvatica

(*fā*-gus sil-*vat*-i-ka)

European beech
Deciduous

Fagus sylvatica, European beech. 10115 NE Thompson St. 6-24-91. 17'4" c, 5'6" d. This is a grand old standard European beech.

Smooth and gray-trunked, this beautiful green-leaved tree can reach 100 feet in height and almost as much in spread. On older trees the bark is said to resemble elephant skin. Native to Europe, this beech has served the human race since the Stone Age. Even the common name is the basis from which our word *book* is derived. There are at least 34 cultivars.

- NW Glisan between 19th Ave. & 20th Ave., 15'6" c, 4'11" d

Fagus sylvatica 'Atropunicea' is a cultivar name under which purple beech and the copper beech are lumped together. The foliage of the latter does not become dark purple, thereby seeming to be copper in hue. Leaf color can vary from tree to tree. These trees attain such a size that it is difficult to do them justice with a photograph.

- 317 SE 52nd Ave., 16'2" c, 5'2" d
- 1579 SE Nehalem St., 15'3" c, 4'10" d (planted about 1892 by Mr. Young soon after he brought his new bride to his new house)
- SE Stark St. & Troutdale Rd., Troutdale, 15' c, 4'9" d (planted 1885)
- 811 NW 20th Ave., 14' c, 4'5" d
- 50 NE 84th Ave., 13'2" c, 4'2" d
- 4333 N Willamette Blvd. (three trees)
- SE 42nd Ave. & Monroe St., Milwaukie (planted by Owen Roberts in 1892)

Fagus sylvatica 'Atropunicea', Copper beech. SE Woodstock Blvd. near Moreland Ln., Reed College. 10-17-91. 18'3" c, 5'10" d. Portland's largest specimen was probably planted between 1912 and 1916 at the president's house (now the music building).

Fagus sylvatica 'Atropunicea', Purple beech. 1719 NE Knott St. 4-25-91. 17'7" c, 5'7" d. The second largest specimen in the city, it was planted about 1916 at the John Linden Bowman home.

Fagus sylvatica 'Atropunicea', Copper beech. Millar Library, Portland State University. 7-10-91. 15'3" c, 4'10" d. Planted around 1890, this tree was saved in the 1980s when the architects designing an addition to the library made one entire side a five-story semicircle to accommodate the tree. To get to the tree from the University's parking lot on SW Broadway & College St., walk 0.5 block west and then 0.5 block north.

Fraxinus latifolia, Oregon ash. X 2205 SW 21st Ave. 7-8-91. 8'9" c, 2'9" d.

Fraxinus latifolia

(*frak*-si-nus la-ti-*fōl*-i-a)

Oregon ash
Deciduous

A member of the olive family, this ash is the only species of the family that is native to Oregon. It inhabits nearly all lowland valleys west of the Cascades from Seattle to northern California, and it is especially abundant in the Willamette Valley. Urbanization, however, has caused much loss of habitat. The species likes moist land, meadows, and swamps. The compound leaves turn bright yellow in the fall. Male and female flowers are borne on separate trees. The seeds (from the female tree only) look something like maple seeds except they are not double. The tree has attractive bark with close-together vertical furrows. It can attain 150 feet, but its more common ultimate height is between 60 and 80 feet. The largest Oregon ash in the state is on Sauvie Island away from a road; in 1975 its girth was 22'11". The wood makes good baseball bats and axe handles, and Native Americans used it to make canoe paddles. It is difficult to find an Oregon ash on the city streets.

- corner SE 23rd Ave. & Lambert St., Westmoreland Park, 7'9" c, 2'6" d, (grove of 11 trees)

Ginkgo biloba

(*gink*-gō bī-*lō*-ba)

Ginkgo or Maidenhair tree

Deciduous

Ginkgo biloba, Ginkgo or Maidenhair tree. Between NE 6th & 7th Ave. & Holladay St. In the middle of the parking lot near the Lloyd Center. 11-3-90. 10'8" c, 3'5" d. The largest ginkgo in Portland, the autumn color of this female tree is seldom spectacular. It was planted possibly in the 1890s. We hope it has a long life.

In 1925 a fossil ginkgo leaf was discovered near Tanner Creek in the Columbia Gorge. In the days of the dinosaurs, this tree grew in the temperate zone, disappearing almost completely during the Ice Age and surviving only in the remote mountains of China. Ginkgo seeds were taken to Japan by Buddhist priests in the sixth century, and Buddhist temples in China and Japan have preserved the species to the present day. Some of the trees in Japan are known to be over 600 years old. They have trunks greater than 14 feet in diameter. The first Westerner to discover the tree was an employee of the Dutch East India Company, Dr. Kaempfer, in 1682. The ginkgo reached Holland by 1737, England by 1754, and Philadelphia by 1784. The oldest ginkgo in the United States was planted in Philadelphia in 1785.

The ginkgo leaf resembles the leaflet of a maidenhair fern, hence the common name. The tree is excellent as a street tree because it is resistant to smoke, dust, wind, and ice, and is free from diseases and injury by insects. It is long-lived and slow growing. Gangly when young, it only takes on its full form in maturity. Trees are either male or female. It is often preferable to plant a male tree because the "fruit" (actually a naked seed or gymnosperm) of the female is malodorous.

Ginkgo trees were introduced in the Portland area in the 1860s. They can be found in several public parks and are a rather common street tree.

- Reed College, in front of the old entrance to the library, 8'4" c, 2'8" d, (two females)
- corner NE 16th Ave. & Brazee St (eight trees)

Ginkgo biloba, Ginkgo or Maidenhair tree. 662 NW Melinda. 11-6-91. 6′c, 1′11″ d. Estimated to have been planted in 1907, the tree shows the full fall color typical of the species.

Gleditsia triacanthos var. *inermis*

(gle-*dit*-si-a trī-a-*kan*-thos in-*er*-mis)

Thornless common honeylocust
Deciduous

This tree's generic name commemorates Gottlieb Gleditsh, a director of the Berlin Botanical Gardens who died in 1786. Native to the central eastern United States, the species has stout, dangerous thorns that make it unsafe to plant as an ornamental. However, one variety, *Gleditsia triacanthos* var. *inermis,* is thornless, hence the name *inermis.* Among the several cultivars, 'Sunburst' rarely reaches a height over 30 feet. It is easy to spot in Portland in the spring and summer.

- 204 NE 44th Ave.
- 2715 NE Weidler St.
- 2393 SW Park Pl.

Gleditsia triacanthos var. *inermis,* Thornless common honeylocust. SW Park Ave. & Jackson St. 4-24-90.

Hydrangea paniculata

(hī-*drān*-jē-a pan-ik-ū-*lā*-ta)

Panicle hydrangea
Deciduous

A tree never more than 25 feet tall, this hydrangea clearly resembles its cousins the shrub hydrangeas. It is originally from Japan and China. Many landscape designers think it is a "monstrosity." The flowers are originally white but from mid-July on they gradually become more and more dark pink, and they stay on the tree for a long period of time.

Somewhat scarce in the Portland area, this small tree has a certain charm.

- 1639 SE Flavel St.

Hydrangea paniculata, Panicle hydrangea. 706 SE Malden St. 10-12-90.

Juglans nigra, Black walnut. NT 17415 SW Walker Rd., Beaverton. 5-16-91. 18'3" c, 5'10" d. This tree may have been one of the 1855 seeds, and it must have been part of an old orchard.

Juglans nigra

(*ju*-glanz *nī*-gra)

Black walnut
Deciduous

Highly prized for its wood, which is used for cabinets, gun stocks, and furniture, few black walnut trees remain in their native habitat, which ranges from Massachusetts to Florida and west to Minnesota and Texas. The wood is so valuable that "walnut rustlers" remove trees by helicopters in midnight operations. Because the tree can attain huge proportions—up to 150 feet high and with a spread not much less than that—this species is generally not a good candidate for a yard or parking strip.

- 7101 SW Beaverton-Hillsdale Hwy., 16'9" c, 5'4" d (planted in 1855 by William and Margaret Baxter from a nut which they purchased from William Barlow, who imported 36 butternuts and 500 black walnuts from the East which he sold to homesteaders for a dollar each)
- 4520 SE 35th Ave., 16'2" c, 5'2" d (only the crown can be seen from the street)
- corner SW Salmon St. & 14th Ave., 14'2" c, 4'6" d
- 1018 Laurel St., Lake Oswego, 14' c, 4'6" d

Juglans regia, English walnut. Reeder Road near Reeder Beach, Sauvie Island. 7-20-91. 12'8" c, 4' d. Planted in the early 1900s, only five trees remain from the original grove.

Juglans regia

(*ju*-glanz *rē*-ji-a)

English walnut
Deciduous

Despite its common name, this species, first mentioned in records from ancient Babylon, is thought to have originated near Persia. The Romans called it "Jupiter's acorn," which in Latin translates into *Jovis glans,* the source of the generic name *Juglans.* Grown for its nuts and wood, and as an ornamental, the English walnut can reach 100 feet in height, although it more often reaches 40 to 60 feet with a comparable spread. Greater Portland has many English walnut trees but few large ones.

- 907 SE Bidwell St. 10'9" c, 3'8" d (probably planted in the 1890s)
- 819 SE Lexington St.
- 2229 NE Clackamas St., 8'7" c, 2'9" d
- 7816 N Haven Ave.
- 540 6th St., Lake Oswego, 9'6" c, 3' d
- 5509 SE 44th Ave., 9' c, 2'10" d

Koelreuteria paniculata, Golden rain tree. 815 & 825 SE Bidwell St. 7-27-90.

Koelreuteria paniculata

(kōl-rū-*tē*-ri-a pan-ik-ū-*lā*-ta)

Golden rain tree
Deciduous

One of the very few yellow-flowering trees, the golden rain tree is a native of China where at one time it was considered sacred. It was named after Joseph Gottlieb Koelreuter, one of the first plant hybridists at the University of Karlsruhe, Germany. It has compound leaves, and the blossoms, when they appear in July, are on long, wide panicles. In the fall, it adds to it attractiveness by producing papery, yellowish-brown, 2-inch-long, lanternlike capsules that remain on the limbs well into September. A relatively small tree—up to 40 feet—it produces an equally wide spread and has a nice round head.

Sellwood residents must have known what a good street tree the golden rain tree would make. It is worth a drive in this neighborhood in mid-April to see the colorful new leaves, again in mid- to late-July to see the show of blossoms, and also in mid-September to see the seeds.

Koelreuteria paniculata, Golden rain tree. 9-13-90. Blossoms and seed pods.

Laburnum anagyroides, Goldenchain tree. 4635 N Concord St. 4-23-90.

Laburnum anagyroides

(la-*ber*-num an-a-jī-*roy*-dēz)

Goldenchain tree
Deciduous

A very small tree (up to 30 feet in height), this species makes a spectacular splash with its golden blooms from spring to early summer. The flower sprays measure about 10 inches in length, hence the common name. The tree is poisonous in all parts if ingested. Like some other members of the pea family, it has leaves that close up at night.

Relatively few of these trees grow in the Portland area, which is a bit mystifying since north from Seattle to Vancouver it is abundant. A drive around Sauvie Island in late April and May will produce a view of several goldenchains.

- 20705 NW Sauvie Island Rd., Sauvie Island
- corner SW Downsview Ct. & Shattuck Rd.
- corner SE Gladstone St. & 33rd Pl.
- 1012 SW Gaines St.

Laegerstroemia indica

(lā-ger-*strē*-mē-a *in*-di-ka)

Crapemyrtle
Deciduous

Laegerstroemia indica, Crapemyrtle. 2377 NW Johnson St. 8-27-90. Dating from the early 1970s, this tree was started from a root cutting of a much older tree that had grown next door and had been cut down.

Tending to be a small tree, the crapemyrtle can achieve a height of about 45 feet. It is abundant in the southern United States and is a common street tree in southern California. Native to China and Korea, it was first identified in India, hence its specific name. Very few crapemyrtles grow in Greater Portland. Those that do, bloom in August, and the flowers, which are crinkled and borne in panicles, are bright and showy.

- 3103 NW Upshur St. (two trees)

Larix decidua

(*lar*-iks dē-*sid*-ū-a)

European larch
Deciduous

Larix decidua, European larch. NW 20th Ave. & Glisan St., Couch Park. 3-23-90. 8' c, 2'6" d. New spring foliage.

A big larch, this conifer can grow to 150 feet high, having horizontal branches with drooping, or pendulous, new growth. New, bright green needles in the spring make quite a show, and in the fall the yellow foliage can take one by surprise. Bare of leaves, the tree looks essentially dead all winter. Many larches of all kinds have lost their lives in the winter—cut down by owners who did not know that some conifers are deciduous. Native to northern and central Europe, it was introduced to the United States in colonial times.

Larix kaempferi, Japanese larch. SW Fischer Rd., Hoyt Arboretum. 11 21 89. Fall foliage Trees planted 1963.

Larix kaempferi

(*lar*-iks *kem*-fer-ī)

Japanese larch
Deciduous

A conifer native to Japan, this tree is a handsome, fast-growing (reaching 130 feet) larch. Spring and fall are the best times to view it. New leaf growth is bright green, and the needles are a brilliant yellow-orange just before they fall in autumn.

Although Japanese larches were introduced early (1861) into the United States, not many of them grow in the Portland area.

Larix occidentalis

(*lar*-iks ox-i-den-*ta*-lis)

Western larch or Tamarack
Deciduous

Larix occidentalis, Western larch or Tamarack. 1975 SW Mongomery Dr. 4-9-91. 6' c, 1'11" d. Planted about 1935 by two little girls who brought it back from Camp Tamarack (near Bend) as a very small tree.

Native to the Pacific Northwest, this tree can grow to over 150 feet tall and 4 feet in diameter in its native habitat. Although it likes moisture, this important timber tree grows only on the eastern slopes of the Cascades to the northern Rocky Mountains. Like all larches and unlike most conifers, it looks quite dead in the winter. The new spring foliage of this tree is highly fragant. Greater Portland has few Western larches on or near its streets.

- 7307 N Villard Ave.
- NT 747 W Powell Blvd., Gresham
- SE Lafayette St. near Powell Blvd., Powell Park (six trees)

Liquidambar styraciflua

(lik-wid-*am*-bar stī-ra-*si*-floo-a)

American sweetgum
Deciduous

Liquidambar styraciflua, American sweetgum. 2617 NE 16th Ave. 11-4-90. 9'10" c, 3'2" d. An example of old trees.

Some people mistake this tree for a maple because of the leaf shape, but the fruit will indicate the difference. Some of the knobby 1.5-inch seed balls stay on the tree and the rest clutter the ground below from fall to spring. Both the generic and common names refer to a quality of the bark that when cut exudes a liquid balm used for perfume, incense, and medicines. The many cultivars of this tree were created mostly for fall leaf color. The bigger, older trees are not usually quite so colorful in the autumn, more often producing muted yellows, reds, and purples. In the wild the sweetgum can attain over 150 feet in height, with a spread of two-thirds to equal the height. Native to the eastern United States, this species provides a leading wood for furniture.

- X 1636 SE Marion St.
- SE Tamarack Ave. & Hickory St.
- 2453 SE Taylor St.
- SE Malden St. & 7th Ave., Sellwood Park, 10' c, 3'2" d (the larger of two trees grown together)

Liquidambar styraciflua, American sweetgum. NW Cornell Rd. & Northrup St. 11-4-90. Vivid fall colors.

Liriodendron tulipifera

(lir-i-ō-*den*-dron tū-li-*pif*-er-a)

Tulip tree or Yellow poplar
Deciduous

Liriodendron tulipifera, Tulip tree or Yellow poplar. 1431 NE Weidler St. 4-23-90. 14'10" c, 4'9" d. The largest of its species in the metropolitan area, this tree was planted in the 1890s by George Nicolai.

One of the tallest native eastern American deciduous species, the tulip tree can reach 200 feet. This valuable timber tree is easy to spot because of its leaf shape, which is almost square. A member of the magnolia family, it has beautiful flowers, most often overlooked because they are greenish yellow and blend with the leaf color.

- 1602 SE 32nd Pl., 13'2" c, 4'2" d
- 3104 SE Gladstone St., 12'11" c, 4'1" d
- 2404 NE Clackamas St., 12'5" c, 3'11" d
- 215 NE Laddington Ct., 12' c, 3'10" d
- 1407 SE Miller St., 11'9" c, 3'9" d
- NE 21st Ave. between Brazee & Thompson St. (row)

Liriodendron tulipifera, Tulip tree or Yellow poplar. 2390 SW Madison St. 11-5-90. 14'2" c, 4'6" d. Fall color.

Liriodendron tulipifera, Tulip tree or Yellow poplar. 5-19-90. The blossoms.

Magnolia acuminata

(mag-*nō*-li-a a-kū-mi-*nā*-ta)

Cucumber tree
Deciduous

Magnolia acuminata, Cucumber tree. Corner NW Glisan St. & 19th Ave. 6-18-91. 10'5" c, 3'4" d. Showing the mature shape.

This species was discovered in Virginia in 1736. Its native habitat extends from New York to Georgia, west to Illinois and Arkansas. When mature, it has a beautiful rounded oval shape and can grow to over 100 feet tall. The lovely, fragrant flowers—yellow-green and bell-shaped—are difficult to see because their color matches the foliage. The young seed pods slightly resemble a cucumber, hence the common name. The Portland area has very few cucumber trees.

• corner SW Fairview Blvd. & Fairview Circus

Magnolia acuminata, Cucumber tree. 5-16-90. The flower.

Magnolia dawsoniana, Dawson's magnolia. SW Cascade Dr., Hoyt Arboretum (near small parking lot). 3-16-91. Taken at the start of its blooming period.

Magnolia dawsoniana

(mag-*nō*-li-a da-*sōn*-i-ān-a)

Dawson's magnolia
Deciduous

Dawson's magnolia, discovered in China in 1908, was named after the first superintendent of Arnold Arboretum in Boston, Massachusetts. The flowers of this tree seem to bloom sideways (rather than facing up or down), and only when they are past their prime do they hang limply downwards. This magnolia is best viewed when the flower buds begin to show color. Many trees wait over 20 years to begin blooming.

Magnolia denudata

(mag-*nō*-li-a de-nū-*dā*-ta)

Yulan magnolia
Deciduous

Magnolia denudata, Yulan magnolia. 8421 SW Macadam Rd. 3-22-91. 6′ c, 1′11″ d. Probably planted when the house was built in 1914.

This relatively small tree from China seldom grows higher than 50 feet. The fragrant, ivory-white flowers appear before the leaves and have nine petals. Early to bloom, the flowers can be quite damaged by late frosts, heavy rains, or strong winds. The species is one of the first flowering trees to be cultivated. Buddhist monks of central China planted this tree in their temple gardens over 1300 years ago. It was introduced into England in 1789.

- NW Westover Rd. & Flanders St., 4′10″ c, 1′6″ d

Magnolia grandiflora

(mag-*nō*-li-a gran-di-*flō*-ra)

Southern magnolia
Evergreen

Magnolia grandiflora, Southern magnolia. X 2822 SW 2nd Ave. 9'6" c, 3' d. Planted in the 1890s, the second largest specimen in the metropolitan area has escaped being downed from impinging development.

A native of southeastern United States and Mississippi's state tree, this magnolia has been in cultivation over 250 years. The leathery leaves are glossy on the top and often slightly fuzzy and brown underneath. The flowers are magnificent: 8 to 12 inches in diameter, creamy-white, and fragrant. The height of this tree can exceed 100 feet with a spread up to 50 feet. Intolerant of very cold (−15°F) weather, the tree can die outright or to the ground.

Large magnolias are plentiful in the Portland area and easy to spot, even in the winter, because of their big, shiny leaves.

- 902 12th St., Oregon City, 10' c, 3'2" d
- 1705 NE Clackamas St., 6'9" c, 2'2" d
- 2941 NW Quimby St.
- 4338 NE Campaign St.
- 2311 NE Thompson St.
- 2390 SW Park Pl. & Douglas Pl. (row of 10, planted by Harry Banfield in 1962 to replace Douglas firs blown down by the Columbus Day storm)

Magnolia grandiflora, Southern magnolia. 6-29-91. The flower.

Magnolia sargentiana var. *robusta*

mag-*nō*-li-a sar-jen-tē-*ā*-na rō-*bus*-ta)

Sargent magnolia
Deciduous

Magnolia sargentiana var. *robusta,* Sargent magnolia. 4343 SW Fairview Blvd. 2-28-91. 5'8" c. 1'10" d. A very rare tree in Portland. On the day after the photograph practically all of the flowers were blown off by heavy wind and rain.

Called the most beautiful of all magnolias when in flower, this magnolia was discovered in western Sichuan, China, in 1908 and introduced to the United States in the form of seeds the same year. It closely resembles Dawson's magnolia, although the latter blooms about two weeks later. Twelve-inch blooms, white on the inside of the petals and pink on the outside, are profuse in late February and early March. The petals have a tendency to curl back when fully expanded. Like a few of its relatives, the Sargent magnolia produces its flowers before the leaves. It can reach a height of 80 feet with a large spread. The tree is very rare in Portland.

Magnolia tripetala

(mag-*nō*-li-a trī-*pet*-al-a)

Umbrella magnolia
Deciduous

Magnolia tripetala, Umbrella magnolia. 1174 SE 53rd Ave. 6-12-91. 5'5" c, 1'9" d.

The original habitat of this native American tree ranges from the central Atlantic states to the southeastern states (excluding Florida). The enormous leaves, clustered near the ends of the branches, measure up to 2 feet in length and one foot in width. The flowers also are large, measuring up to 10 inches in diameter. This tree rarely exceeds 35 feet in height, although it can attain over 80 feet. It grows best in moist places, but is rare in the Portland area.

Magnolia tripetala, Umbrella magnolia. 6-17-91. The flower.

Magnolia × *soulangiana,* Saucer magnolia. 735 SE Umatilla St. 3-19-90. 9′ c, 2′10″ d. Planted before 1920, this tree speaks for itself.

Magnolia × *soulangiana*

(mag-*nō*-li-a soo-lan-jē-*ā*-na)

Saucer magnolia
Deciduous

A cross between *Magnolia denudata* and *M. quinquepeta* (both natives of China), this hybrid first flowered in 1826 in France. The tree, which reaches 30 feet in height and in spread, is an early bloomer among the magnolias and sometimes can be nipped by a late spring frost. The many cultivars include some with enormous flowers, others with dark purplish flowers, and one with white flowers called 'Alba Superba'. Most often the petal number of the saucer magnolia is nine and usually the inside of the petal is whitish. The shape of the flower is campanulate.

A drive around Greater Portland sometime from mid-March to the first week of April will produce views of many saucer magnolias. Because of their relatively small size they easily fit into front or side yards.

- 1807 SW Vista Ave. ('Alba Superba')
- 2357 NW Irving St.
- 1041 SW Vista Ave.

Malus floribunda

(*mal*-us flō-ri-*bun*-da)

Japanese flowering crabapple
Deciduous

A tree that lives up to its scientific name each spring: the blossoms are abundant! The flower buds are red but the bloom is nearly white and subtle overall, tending to make the tree look washed-out when photographed. The tree, which was introduced from Japan in 1862, is a favorite because of its profuse flowering and because it is easy to grow.

Many of these trees flourish in Greater Portland and quite often are planted as a group by the edge of a highway or at large intersections.

- along SE McLoughlin Blvd. in the vicinity of 17th Ave.
- NE corner of the eastside approach to the Broadway bridge

Malus floribunda, Japanese flowering crabapple. SE 60th Ave. & Stark St. 4-2-91. One of several groups of this crabapple in the city.

Malus pumila 'Yellow Bellflower'

(*mal*-us *pū*-mil-a *yel*-ō *bel*-flau-er))

Yellow bellflower apple
Deciduous

Malus pumila 'Yellow Bellflower'. SW Dosch Park Ln. 4-9-90. This ancient tree still blooms well and bears fruit.

This is the oldest, living, grafted standard fruit variety in the western United States. Originally a colonial fruit tree, the bellflower moved West with the pioneers, reaching the Oregon Territory in 1847 in Henderson Luelling's wagonload of fruit trees. Albert Kelly, one of the early settlers, planted bellflowers in the orchard on his Donation Land Claim. Years later, a Kelly family member who remembered playing among the trees as a little girl also recalled that the trees were from the Luelling and Meek nursery in Milwaukie.

One of those bellflowers, a first-generation descendant of the trees carried in Luelling's wagon, possibly budded in 1848 and is still living today (see photo). It owes its longevity to Mrs. Henry E. Dosch, who purchased the Kelly place in 1888. Thanks to the effort of her horticulturist husband and his daughter Margueritte Campbell, the long-neglected orchard was tended. In 1901 Colonel Dosch reported on the state of horticulture in Oregon, mentioning "apple trees standing on my own grounds near Portland and planted nearly fifty years ago—Baldwins, Spitzenbergs, Gloria Mundi, and Bellflower." In 1978 the Home Orchard Society installed a plaque at the base of the ancient bellflower, and the society has since cared for the tree.

Malus pumila is native to southeastern Europe and central Asia and widely naturalized in North America. Several *Malus* species are cultivated for their handsome flowers or fruits. Best known are the myriad varieties of eating and cooking apples. The bellflower, a large, handsome winter apple, is pale lemon-yellow and a favorite for making pies.

Malus × *purpurea*

(*mal*-us per-*per*-ē-a)

Purple crabapple
Deciduous

Crabapples are impressive in the spring when planted as allées, but blossoming lasts a little over a week, so it does not pay to dally. Greater Portland abounds with flowering crabs, but little has been written about them.

Malus × *purpurea*, Purple crabapple. NW 22nd Ave. & Flanders St. 4-9-90.

Metasequoia glyptostroboides

(met-a-sē-*kwoy*-a glip-tō-strō-*boy*-dēz)

Dawn redwood
Deciduous

Like the larch, the dawn redwood is a deciduous conifer. Fossils of this tree were discovered in Japan in 1941, the same year the tree was discovered alive in central China by T. Kan, a Chinese forester. The species actually had been growing and reproducing itself in a remote part of Sichuan Province since the time of the dinosaurs. Seeds first came to the United States in 1944, brought by the Arnold Arboretum of Boston. Some of them were given to Hoyt Arboretum in 1948, which means that Portland has some of the oldest dawn redwoods in the country. One of Hoyt Arboretum's trees grew the first cone ever produced in the Western Hemisphere in 50 million years. John Bacher and Bill Robinson are two Portland plant enthusiasts who had early success producing this tree from cuttings. A fast grower whose ultimate height is up to 200 feet, the dawn redwood belongs to the same family as the sequoias and redwoods and is most attractive when in its new bright-green spring leafing phase.

- X 2534 SW Ravensview Dr. (planted in 1965 as a young plant)
- 3515 N Lombard St. (planted in 1948 from seed)
- 666 C St., Lake Oswego
- 0615 SW Palatine Hill Rd., entrance to Lewis & Clark College

Metasequoia glyptostroboides, Dawn redwood. SE 27th Ave. at foot of Rex St., East-moreland Golf Course. 4-4-90 & 11-20-89. Spring and fall foliage.

Metasequoia glyptostroboides, Dawn redwood. 7521 SE 30th Ave. 4-25-91. 5'4" c, 2' d. The trunk at close view.

Nyssa sylvatica

(*nis*-a sil-*vat*-i-ka)

Tupelo, Sour gum, or Black gum
Deciduous

Nyssa sylvatica, Tupelo, Sour gum, Black gum. SE 7th Ave. & Malden St., Sellwood Park (near parking lot). 10-23-90. 7'9" c, 2'6" d.

The tupelo is native from Maine to Texas. A beautiful tree, especially in its fall colors, which range from yellow and red to purple, it can grow to over 100 feet high, but more likely ranges from 30 to 50 feet. In the summer its leaves are a lustrous dark green. At times the dark gray bark appears almost black; it looks like an alligator hide. The fruit is bluish black, somewhat resembling olives, and is attractive to birds. It is a very rare tree along Greater Portland streets—a pity.

Oxydendrum arboreum

(ok-si-*den*-drum ar-*bō*-rē-um)

Sourwood
Deciduous

Oxydendrum arboreum, Sourwood. 2204 SE 35th Pl. 11-13-91. 3'5" c, 1'1" d. The beautiful autumn leaves of this tree have already begun to fall.

An outstanding native American tree, its original habitat stretches from Virginia to Florida, Ohio, and Louisiana. It blooms in mid- to late-summer with white, urn-shaped, fragrant panicles resembling the flowers of the shrub *Pieris japonica* (andromeda). A slow grower, the sourwood takes many years to achieve its mature height of around 40 feet. Fall leaf colors are superb—brilliant scarlet to plum. Greater Portland has many small, shrub-size sourwoods, but trees of the size in the photograph are very rare.

- 4305 SE Raymond St., 5'2" c, 1'6" d (a low trunk split exaggerates the girth of this tree)

Paulownia tomentosa

(paw-*lō*-ni-a tō-men-*tō*-sa)

Empress tree or Paulownia
Deciduous

Paulownia tomentosa, Empress tree or Paulownia. NW 20th Ave. & Hoyt St., Couch Park. 4-21-90. 15'2" c, 4'10" d. Planted at the home of Henry Hewett by either Captain John Couch, after an expedition to the Orient, or by 19th-century Chinese immigrants.

A fast-growing tree that can gain as much as 8 to 10 feet in one year, this native of China was named by the German botanist Philipp Siebold after Anna Pavlovna, daughter of the Russian Czar Paul I. Until recently, the Japanese traditionally planted an empress tree at the birth of a baby girl, then when she married, they cut it down to make a chest for her dowry. The Japanese wooden sandals (*geta*) are also made from this light, fine-grained wood. In the United States the paulownia now grows wild from southern New York to Georgia. The time to view the tree is when it is in full bloom, usually from mid-April to mid-May. The violet-colored, vanilla-scented flowers appear before the leaves are visible. Paulownias are rather abundant in the Portland area.

- 7103 SE Yamhill St., 16' c, 5'1" d
- 1015 SE 15th Ave., 11' c, 3'6" d
- 5230 SE 17th Ave.
- 537 Country Club Rd., Lake Oswego
- 7021 N Curtis Ave.
- corner of N Woolsey Ave. & Lombard St., Columbia Park
- SW King St. & Kings Ct.

Photinia serrulata, Chinese photinia. 3182 SE Lake Rd., Milwaukie. 4-10-91. 7'6" c, 2'5" d. This enormous specimen is at the last home of Oregon's famous Abigail Scott Duniway.

Photinia serrulata

(fō-*tin*-i-a ser-ū-*lā*-ta)

Chinese photinia
Evergreen

This plant frequently reaches no more than shrub size and is often used to make a hedge. It can, however, be trimmed and shaped into a small tree reaching over 50 feet. When it blooms the tree is spectacular. The white flowers, in flattened clusters, measure up to 7 inches across. While they do not have a pleasant odor, their profusion and contrast with the young foliage more than make up for this shortcoming.

Although this tree is rather rare in the Portland area, its relatives, *Photinia glabra* and *P.* × *fraseri,* both shrubs with bright red new leaf growth in the spring that are much used for highway plantings, are common and bloom about three weeks later than Chinese photinia.

- 2533 NW Savier St.
- SW Front Ave. & Meade St. (on the freeway approach, so look quickly)
- 2135 NE 20th Ave.
- 1112 SW 20th Ave.
- X 10 SW Ash St.

Picea abies

(pī-*sē-a ā*-bēz)

Norway spruce
Evergreen

Picea abies, Norway spruce. 744 5th St., Lake Oswego. 3-28-91. 15'7" c, 5' d.

The Norway spruce is native to northern and central Europe, where it is the dominant species in the Black Forest. It was introduced to the United States in colonial times. It can attain a height of 150 feet. The enormous cones of this tree, measuring more than 8 inches long, are purple or green when young and light brown when mature. Because of its pendant, sweeping branches, this tree has often been used in groups as windbreaks. There are several cultivars of the Norway spruce with slight differences (e.g., some have more pendant branches than others), which make identification rather confusing.

- 1852 SW Highland Rd.
- 2156 SW Laurel St.

Picea breweriana

(pī-*sē*-a brew-er-ē-*ā*-na)

Brewer spruce
Evergreen

Picea breweriana, Brewer spruce. X 2525 SW Montgomery Dr. 7-20-91. A young but handsome tree.

Found wild only in the Klamath-Siskiyou Mountains of southwestern Oregon and northern California, the Brewer spruce prefers moist, north-facing slopes and canyons, and an elevation of 4000 to 8000 feet. It attains less than 100 feet in height but stands out from other conifers because of its drooping, almost perpendicular secondary branches. Since it grows slowly, it can be considered for a small city garden. Named for Professor W. H. Brewer, the botanist with Whitney's California surveying party of 1860–1864, this tree remains very rare on Greater Portland streets, but is something to behold, even when it is relatively young.

Picea pungens, Colorado spruce. 720 NW Warrenton Terr. 6-27-91. 6′ c, 1′11″ d. One of the largest in the metropolitan area, this spruce was probably planted soon after the house was built in 1929/1930.

Picea pungens

(pī-*sē*-a *pun*-jenz)

Colorado spruce
Evergreen

A very popular landscape tree in the Portland area, especially in its "blue" form, the Colorado spruce is native to the southwestern Rocky Mountains. Both Colorado and Utah claim it as their state tree. The stiff, sharp needles are typical of spruces, and the ultimate height is about 150 feet with a 20- to 30-foot spread.

Colorado spruces are so common on front lawns in the Portland area that they are often ignored.

Picea sitchensis

(pī-*sē*-a sit-*chen*-sis)

Sitka spruce
Evergreen

Picea sitchensis, Sitka spruce. 785 3rd St., Lake Oswego. 6-27-91. 7'2" c, 2'3" d. Planted in the 1920s.

The Sitka spruce tree is native to the Northwest, found close to the coast from northern California to Kodiak Island, Alaska. In the mountains of Washington and British Columbia, Sitka spruces extend up the major river valleys, but from the Columbia River south the tree is strictly coastal. It can become massive. The largest specimen in the United States, near Seaside, Oregon, measures 52.5 feet in circumference and 216 feet in height, and has a crown spread of 93 feet. Bald eagles by the thousands use these trees for roosting. The high resonant qualities of the wood make it useful for musical instruments. The tree's new growth, bright green at first, becomes bluish green by early summer, giving an overall pleasing appearance. Introduced into Britain in the early 1800s by David Douglas, the famous Scottish botanist, the Sitka spruce is now that country's most widely planted tree.

Probably because it is coastal in Oregon, few Sitka spruces are found in Greater Portland. None is as large as the trees found at the beach.

- 417 SE 76th Ave. 5'8" c, 1'10" d
- at the southwest end of the Metro zoo overpass of Highway 26 (top removed)

Pinus contorta

(*pī*-nus con-*tōrt*-a)

Lodgepole, Coast,
or Shore pine
Evergreen

Pinus contorta, Lodgepole pine. X 560 4th St., Lake Oswego. 6-27-91. 6'7" c, 2'1" d.

This pine grows in two forms, one of which can be seen in profusion along the coast from Alaska to Baja, California, where it is small and twisted, and the other of which can be found inland in the mountains, stretching from the Yukon Territory east to the Black Hills of South Dakota and south into California. Biologists puzzle over the fact that one species can tolerate such a vast range of environments. The coast form is known as coast or shore pine and the inland form as lodgepole pine, first called this by Lewis and Clark when they noticed that Native Americans would travel long distances to gather these trees for poles to support their lodges.

This is the only native pine to have needles in bundles of two. The cones are also distinctive, being 1.5 to 2 inches long and covered with prickles. Typically, they face away from the end of the branch. Many of the cones do not open until subjected to heat (fire or hot sun), providing this tree a reproductive head start after a forest fire. Also, it is typical for the cones to remain on the tree for several years. Height of this tree depends on environment; under very favorable conditions it can reach 200 feet, but one has only to look at the coast pine growing in sand, salt air, and gale winds to see the other end of the height scale.

Greater Portland has many small lodgepole pines. The largest in Oregon is in the Winema National Forest near Crater Lake; in 1983 it measured 12'4" in circumference.

- 10660 SE 21st St., Ledding Library, Milwaukie, 6'8" c, 2'1" d

Pinus coulteri

(*pī*-nus *kōl*-ter-ī)

Coulter, Big-cone,
or Pitch pine
Evergreen

Pinus coulteri, Coulter or Big-cone pine. 5306 SE 37th Ave. 7-9-91. 8′6″ c, 2′8″ d.

As one of its common names implies, this pine has big cones; the heaviest of all the world's pines, each cone can be 8 to 14 inches long and weigh 4 to 8 pounds. The tree is three-needled, and the needles are stiff, sharp-pointed, and 8 to 12 inches long. With an ultimate height of about 70 feet, it is one of the shorter pines. Thomas Coulter, the Irish botanist and physician, discovered the big-cone pine in 1831. Its native habitat ranges from central to north Baja, California. It likes dry, rocky slopes in foothills and mountains, and it withstands heat, drought, and wind very well. A trip to see this tree is worth it—the cones are incredible!

- 5352 SE 37th Ave., 8′7″ c, 2′9″ d

Pinus densiflora

(*pī*-nus den-si-*flō*-ra)

Japanese red pine
Evergreen

Pinus densiflora, Japanese red pine. 10660 SE 21st Ave., Ledding Library, Milwaukie. 2-23-91. 10'11" c, 3'6" d.

A handsome two-needled pine with orange-red, flaky bark, as its common name implies, this tree is native to Japan. The form one sees most often is not the single-trunked, 100-foot-high tree, but rather a shorter, multitrunked cultivar called 'Umbraculifera'. This variety has an umbrellalike head and grows to be less than 50 feet tall. A compact form called 'Tanyosho Pine' seldom attains even 9 feet. All three varieties have many cones that remain open on the tree for 2 to 3 years.

- corner NE 39th Ave. & Couch St. (two trees)

Pinus monticola

(*pī*-nus mon-*ti*-kō-la)

Western white pine
Evergreen

Pinus monticola, Western white pine. 1726 SE 24th Ave. 5-8-91. 10′ c, 3′2″ d.

Native to the western United States from sea level to timberline, this tree is one of the four 5-needled pines that grows in the Pacific Northwest. Idaho claims it as the state tree. Attaining a height of over 200 feet in the wild, this handsome pine has needles about 4 inches in length and cones that are from 5 to 10 inches long and 2.5 to 3 inches wide. At the end of each cone scale there is much white pitch.

It is unusual to find Western white pine growing in the city.

Pinus nigra

(pī-nus nī-gra)

Austrian pine
Evergreen

Pinus nigra, Austrian pine. 1425 SW 20th Ave. 12-16-89. 9'2" c, 2'11" d. Planted sometime in the last century by Henry Miller, one of the first nursery owners in Portland.

The Austrian pine is a very hardy tree, withstanding urban conditions, dryness, heat, and cold. Its stiff needles make it a good windbreak tree. It becomes more handsome with age when the bark turns dark gray with a tinge of pink, and is deeply fissured. The ultimate height can be over 70 feet. The needles come in bundles of two and are 4 to 6 inches long, while the cones are 2 to 3 inches long. Henry Miller introduced this pine to the local nursery trade in 1860.

- SW Jefferson St. at the side of the Portland Art Museum, 7'1" c, 2'3" d
- 1144 SE 55th Ave., 8'10" c, 2'10" d
- 5511 SE Hawthorne Blvd.

Pinus ponderosa, Ponderosa pine. 4504 SW Shattuck Rd. 11-16-90. 15' c, 4'9" d.

Pinus ponderosa

(*pī*-nus pon-der-*ō*-sa)

Ponderosa pine
Evergreen

A pine of ponderous bulk, it is a native of the Rockies, from British Columbia to Mexico, and of the Pacific Northwest. It was discovered (near the middle Columbia River close to present-day Colville, Washington) and given its species name by the botanist-explorer David Douglas. It is the state tree of Montana. A two- to three-needled pine, the needles vary from 5 to 11 inches in length. The older ponderosas have distinctive bark that looks like the Grand Canyon from 35,000 feet in the air: pinkish, yellowish, and broken into large, flat, superficially scaly plates separated by deep, irregular fissures. The cones, 3 to 6 inches long, are terminal, from one to five together, and sessile. Each scale has a stout, recurved prickle. The ponderosa is the most important pine in western North America. In the wild it attains heights of up to 250 feet with a spread of only 25 to 30 feet. The largest in Oregon, near the Deschutes River south of Bend, is nearly 9 feet in diameter.

Ponderosa seeds made their way from the Rockies to the upper end of the Willamette Valley by way of the Missoula Floods from 50,000 to 12,000 years ago. They found hospitable soil and climate in such places as the Tualatin Valley. There are many groves of 300-year-old ponderosas in the Beaverton and Tigard areas. The tallest and probably the oldest (some 300 to 500 years old) are in unurbanized parts of Beaverton. Scatterings of big, old trees can be found also near Gresham and Oregon City.

- SW Millikan Blvd. near 154th Terr., Beaverton (a grove)
- 605 Harrison St., Oregon City, 15' c, 4'9" d (three trees)
- 3437 NE 29th Ave., 12'11" c, 4'1" d
- 5060 SE Lake Rd., Milwaukie, 12'2" c, 3'10" d
- 5015 SW Dosch Rd., 11'7" c, 3'8" d
- X 1987 SW Montgomery Pl., 10'6" c, 3'4" d
- along both sides of Highway 217, Tigard

Pinus ponderosa, Ponderosa pine. SW Millikan Blvd. near Murray Rd., Beaverton, Tualatin Valley Nature Park. 3-8-91. 9'8" c, 3'1" d.

Pinus ponderosa, Ponderosa pine. 5-4-91. Male (above) and female (below) "flowers."

Platanus occidentalis

(*plat*-a-nus ok-si-den-*ta*-lis)

American planetree or
American sycamore
Deciduous

Platanus occidentalis, American planetree or American Sycamore. X 4234 SE 33rd Pl. 5-22-91. 13'9" c, 4'5" d.

The sycamore, one of the biggest native deciduous trees in North America, frequently attains a height of 100 feet—although it can grow to 175 feet—a diameter up to 10 feet, and a very wide-spreading crown. When the red-brown, scaly bark exfoliates, it exposes lighter colored inner layers. The fruit, a single globular head of seeds, hangs on a stem 3 to 6 inches long. Falling flakes of bark, seeds, leaves, and twigs all contribute to making this a messy tree. With a native habitat extending from Maine to Minnesota and south to northern Florida and Texas, the sycamore is not nearly so common in Portland as is the London planetree. An easy way to tell the difference is that latter has more than two connected seedheads.

- corner NW 19th Ave. & Flanders St.
- SW 2nd Ave. between Pine & Oak Sts. (row)
- NE Knott St. between 16th & 17th Aves. (row of eight trees)
- SE 7th Ave. between Bidwell & Lambert Sts.

Platanus × *acerifolia*

(*plat*-a-nus ā-ser-e-*fō*-lē-a)

London planetree
Deciduous

Platanus × *acerifolia*, London planetree. SE 39th Ave. & Stephens St. 9-25-90. 25'3" c, 8' d.

A hybrid between the American sycamore (*Platanus occidentalis*) and the oriental planetree (*P. orientalis*), the first record of this hybrid dates back to 1663 when a tree, possibly the first hybrid of garden origin, was found growing in London. John Tradescant, who with his father was gardener to Charles I of England, made a trip to Virginia in 1637 and returned with *P. occidentalis* seeds, which he planted near an already-established *P. orientalis* from southeastern Europe. The two species produced offspring—the London planetree.

Now a common tree in Europe, the London planetree is frequently found heavily pollarded and forming allées in French cities and towns. Because it can attain a height of 150 feet and a spread of 65 to 80 feet, it needs plenty of space to reach its potential, unless it is pruned annually. A true city tree capable of thriving in all kinds of pollution, the London planetree grows near many of Portland's streets.

The Farrell sycamore (see photo) was declared a historic landmark by the Portland City Council in 1973. In 1880 Senator J. N. Dolph gave the young tree to Sylvester Farrell, who planted it where it is today, which was then beside his house. A city commissioner and water bureau head, Farrell was born in 1833 and came to Portland in 1867.

- 1816 SE 21st Ave., 17'4" c, 5'6" d
- block bounded by SW 13th Ave., Yamhill St., 12th Ave., Taylor St. (24 trees on periphery)

Platanus × *acerifolia,* London planetree. Corner SW Main St. & Park Ave. 10-7-90. 13′ c, 4′2″d. The Farrell sycamore. The first historic tree recognized by Portland.

Populus nigra 'Italica', Lombardy poplar. SE 17th Ave. & Taylor St., Summers Park. 9-13-90. 21' c, 6'8" d. This tree, a solitary specimen, has a remarkable trunk.

Populus nigra 'Italica'

(*pop*-ū-lus *nī*-gra i-*tal*-i-ka))

Lombardy poplar
Deciduous

This unmistakable poplar can reach 130 feet in height, is columnar in shape, and very little of the trunk is bare of limbs. Its origin remains unclear, but it is thought to have occurred as a mutant in Italy in the early 1700s. The tree is widely cultivated for avenues as windbreaks, and as boundary indicators. The limbs tend to break easily and the species does not live long, relatively speaking.

The Portland area has many of these trees, mostly in rows.

- SE McLoughlin Blvd. near Bybee Blvd. (row)
- NW 18th Ave. between Burnside & Couch (row)
- SE 36th Ave. & Rhine St. (row)
- 4th St. between A & B Sts., Lake Oswego, 17'7" c, 5'7" d

Populus tremuloides

(*pop*-ū-lus trem-ū-*loy*-dēz)

Quaking aspen
Deciduous

Unlike its cousins the cottonwoods, the aspen is a relatively small tree, usually not exceeding 50 feet in height. Its leaves are dark green above and silvery beneath, and, because the leaf stalks are long and flat, the slightest breeze causes the leaves to tremble and quake. In the fall the foliage becomes a brilliant gold. One of the few trees that ranges from the Atlantic to the Pacific Coast, the quaking aspen has one of the widest distributions of any tree in North America. Although the aspen is more common east of the Cascades and in the Rockies than in the Willamette Valley, the Portland area can call it a native. A few native groves remain in Beaverton.

- SW Watson Ave. between 5th & 6th Sts., Beaverton

Populus tremuloides, Quaking aspen. SW Millikan Blvd near 154th Terr., Beaverton. 11-13-91. Preserved by the architects of a large office complex.

Populus trichocarpa

(*pop*-ū-lus trī-kō-*kar*-pa)

Black cottonwood
Deciduous

Populus trichocarpa, Black cottonwood. 1217 Laurel St., Lake Oswego. 6-27-91. It was impossible to find the largest. This tree is typical.

The black cottonwood, one of the Northwest's native trees, is the largest of North American cottonwoods, achieving heights of over 200 feet and diameters of over 9 feet. Some specimens are 200 years old. The species grows all along the Pacific Slope from south-central Alaska to southern California, but it reaches optimum development in the Pacific Northwest. This tree stores such large quantities of water that if one is cut down, water gushes out from the stump. Males and females are separate trees; only the females make the "cotton." In the spring these trees produce a marvelous fragrance from both their flowers and new foliage. A drive with the windows open along the Columbia Gorge just east of Portland or along the Willamette River just south of Portland in about mid-April, for example, will provide much pleasure for the nose. The fall foliage is a bright yellow.

This tree is not exactly a street or garden tree and should never be considered for these sites. Look for these giants throughout the metropolitan area, especially along any river or stream. The largest black cottonwood in Oregon is in Willamette Mission State Park. In 1984 its circumference was 26'3''.

- NT Willamette River, at the SE end of the Hawthorne bridge; one trunk is 7' c, 2'3'' d (three-trunked tree)

Populus × *canadensis,* Carolina poplar. 3945 & 3957 NE Couch St. 5-19-90. 16' c, 5'1" d. The houses in the background were built around 1911 and are reported to be the first in Laurelhurst.

Populus × *canadensis*

(*pop*-ū-lus kan-a-*den*-sis)

Carolina poplar
Deciduous

A cross between the Eastern cottonwood (*Populus deltoides*) and the Lombardy poplar (*P. nigra*) made the Carolina poplar. It is more vigorous than either parent and only male trees are propagated to avoid the messy "cotton."

Between 1900 and 1915 the Portland nursery trade must have really pushed this tree for street plantings, probably because it would "make a good shade tree" and it was fast growing. There are several of these giants in the city, all along the street in front of houses built near the turn of the century. It is not a tree for the parking strip—the roots are thirsty and strong, and can manage to even break through cement, either that of the sidewalk or the sewer.

- 2620 SE 43rd Ave., 15'4" c, 4'11" d
- 311 NE Laddington Ct., 14'9" c, 4'8" d
- 35 SE 32nd Ave.
- 4362 SE Flanders St.

Prunus avium, Sweet cherry. 3536 E Burnside St. 4-5-90. Gorgeous when in bloom, its fruit is bright red. It is a "volunteer" of the 1940s.

Prunus avium

(*proo*-nus *ā*-vi-um)

Sweet or Mazzard cherry
Deciduous

Although its fruit is small and ranges from light to dark red, this is the species from which most of our eating cherries are derived. It is from Europe and western Asia and has been cultivated since ancient times. One of the hardiest cherries, it provides rootstock for grafting both fruiting and flowering cherry trees.

Prunus avium 'Bing', the Bing cherry, was developed in the 1870s by the early Oregon horticulturist and grower Seth Lewelling, who owned a nursery in Milwaukie next to his home. Lewelling named the cherry after his Chinese foreman, Ah Sit Bing. Greater Portland has many, many of these cherry trees with delicious dark red fruit.

Prunus avium 'Royal Ann', the Royal Ann cherry, is another popular cultivar. In Scott Park next to Milwaukie's Ledding Library stands a Royal Ann cherry tree that is a remnant of the orchards set out by Lewelling in the late 1800s. It is likely that the scion for this Royal Ann was taken from one of the trees carried across the plains in 1847 by Seth's brother Henderson Luelling (the brothers chose to spell their last name differently).

- 4205 SE Ramona St., 12'10" c, 4'1" d (house built in 1912 and the tree probably planted soon after)

Prunus avium 'Bing', Bing cherry. 5907 SE 39th Ave.
4 4 90. Old and attractive.

Prunus avium 'Royal Ann',
Royal Ann cherry. 10660 SE
21st Ave., Scott Park,
Milwaukie. 3-23-90. 10'7" c,
3'4" d.

Prunus domestica

(*proo*-nus dō-*mes*-ti-ka)

European plum
Deciduous

The background of this species, which probably originated in southwestern Asia, is a bit hazy. Of the many cultivars, 'Damson', 'Greengage', and Italian prune are known best to most people.

Prunus domestica, European plum. 434 NW 19th Ave. 3-15-90. Planted in the 1890s.

Prunus serrulata

(*proo*-nus ser-ū-*lā*-ta)

Japanese flowering cherry
Deciduous

This cherry has over 120 cultivars, the origin of many having been lost to antiquity. The cultivars are usually grafted onto *Prunus avium* at about 4 to 6 feet from the ground (evident by a bulge in the trunk). Japan is the country of origin of many cultivars, hence the Japanese names.

The Portland area is abundant with flowering cherries in the spring. There are allées, rows, and single spectacular displays. It would take a book by itself to do an adequate job of listing all that Portland has.

- Westmoreland Park, usually in mid-March (many cultivars bordering the lake)
- 17426 NW Lucy Reeder Rd., Sauvie Island (a grove of about 50 trees)
- NW 19th Ave. between Flanders St. & Glisan St. (row)

Prunus serrulata, 'Kwanzan', Japanese flowering cherry. 3612 to 3632 NE Flanders St. 4-22-91.

Prunus serrulata
'Akebono', Japanese
flowering cherry. A St.
between 5th & 6th Sts.,
Lake Oswego. 3-22-91.

Prunus serrulata 'Shirotae'
or 'Mt. Fuji', Japanese
flowering cherry. Corner
SW Wright Ave. &
Tichner Dr. 3-26-91.

Prunus serrulata, Japanese
flowering cherry. Corner
NW Albemarle Terr. &
Cumberland Rd. 3-30-90.
No one has been able to
identify the variety of this
tree, planted in the early
1900s.

Prunus subhirtella 'Pendula'

(*proo*-nus sub-her-*tel*-a *pen*-dūl-a)

Weeping Japanese cherry
Deciduous

Introduced to the United States from Japan in 1894, this cultivar is very long lived. One in Japan is known to be over 1000 years old, and another measures over 32 feet in circumference.

Greater Portland has many large and attractive weeping Japanese cherries. Unlike many of the flowering cherries, this cultivar, with white and pink varieties, often grows without having been grafted.

- 811 NW 20th Ave.
- 1424 NE 33rd Ave.
- 4215 N Winchell St. (six in the parking strip)
- Milwaukie Jr. High School (four trees)

Prunus subhirtella 'Pendula', Weeping Japanese cherry. 1111 SW Vista Ave. 3-23-90.

Pseudotsuga menziesii

(soo-dō-*soo*-ga men-*zē*-sē-ī)

Douglas fir
Evergreen

Oregon's state tree, the Douglas fir, is a native of the West from the Rocky Mountains to the Pacific Coast and from British Columbia to Mexico. The most valuable timber tree in the United States, it grows to over 300 feet in height in its native habitat and lives up to 2000 years. The virgin stands of Douglas fir are diminishing to the point of almost non-existence.

The tree's specific name (which it acquired from taxonomists only in 1950) honors Dr. Archibald Menzies, who discovered this species in 1792 on the coast of Vancouver Island when he was accompanying Captain George Vancouver on Pacific coastal explorations. Three decades later another explorer-botanist, David Douglas, found the species in Oregon country, hence the common name. Not a true fir, its common name is sometimes written as one word to signify this fact.

The cone, which hangs down and has three-pronged bracts sticking out from between the cone scales, is the most obvious key to identification. Many birds and mammals depend on the Douglas fir for food and shelter. We lose them when we lose the trees.

A rough estimate of the number of Douglas firs in the metropolitan area is one for every three people. The largest specimens are in Forest Park, away from the streets.

A Douglas fir in Lake Oswego, called the Peg Tree (see photo), was used as a lanternpost for town meetings back when the town of Oswego was all to the east of what is now State Street. When Leonard Street was widened in the late 1800s, the town saved this Douglas fir and, although it has lost its top a couple of times, it is a fine, well-cared-for specimen.

The largest Douglas fir in the United States was identified in 1991 in Coos County, Oregon. Reaching 338 feet in height, it is over 34 feet in circumference.

Pseudotsuga menziesii, Douglas fir. 141 Leonard St., Lake Oswego. 6-18-91. 15'6"c, 4'11"d. The Peg Tree.

Pyrus calleryana

(*pi*-rus kal-er-ē-*ā*-na)

Pyrus calleryana 'Chanticleer', Callery pear. NE Weidler St. between 13th & 15th Aves. 3-23-90, 11-4-90. The beautiful spring blossoms and the handsome red foliage of fall. These trees and many red maples replaced 185 London planetrees around the Lloyd Center.

Callery pear
Deciduous

The callery pear is native to China and was introduced in the United States in 1908 to breed fireblight resistance into fruiting pears. Although this goal never came to pass, the callery pear has proved to be an outstanding ornamental tree. Both the callery and its cultivars (about 4 to 5 varieties) make fine street and lawn trees, full of white blossoms in the spring and colorful red foliage in the fall. The fruit is insignificant and does not pose a litter problem. Ultimate height for the callery is 50 feet and about 35 feet for the cultivars.

- SE Linn St. between 13th & 15th Aves. (row)

Pyrus communis, Pear. Behind Milwaukie Junior High School by the RR tracks. 3-30-90. 8'2" c, 2'7" d. Planted in the 1880s, this tree is believed to be a 'Seckel'.

Pyrus communis

(*pi*-rus kom-*mū*-nis)

Pear
Deciduous

A native of Europe and western Asia, the pear has been long cultivated and hybridized for its fruit. By way of birds and other animals the seeds are dispersed in the wild. *Pyrus* species in general are early bloomers, and lend themselves well to espalier techniques.

Greater Portland has many pears of various cultivated varieties. It is difficult to distinguish pear trees from apple trees until each bears fruit.

- X 1853 SW Highland Rd. (10 espaliered against a fence)

Quercus bicolor

(*kwer*-kus *bī*-kol-er)

Swamp white oak
Deciduous

Quercus bicolor, Swamp white oak. W Burnside St. & SW 19th Ave. 6-26-91. 7'10" c, 2'6" d. Located behind a fountain erected in 1911 to commemorate David Campbell, Portland's fire chief from 1893–1911 who died while fighting a fire, this tree was probably planted the same year.

As its common name implies, this oak likes a moist soil, but it can also survive in drier conditions. Native to the northeastern United States, it is a slow-growing tree, attaining a height of 50 to 70 feet. The leaves are a shiny dark green above and silvery white underneath, with rounded lobes. The tree typically produces acorns in pairs on long stalks. Its bark is scaly, flaky, coarsely ridged, and furrowed. It is a rare tree in Greater Portland.

Quercus garryana

(*kwer*-kus ger-rē-*ā*-na)

Oregon white or Garry oak
Deciduous

Quercus garryana, Oregon white or Garry oak. SW Park Ave. near Salmon St. 1 7 90. 9'9" c, 3'1" d. The Strong oak.

David Douglas, the noted Scottish botanist, discovered this tree in the 1820s and named it for Nicholas Garry of the Hudson's Bay Company, who helped Douglas in his explorations. The Oregon white oak grows along the southwestern coast of Vancouver Island, in a few scattered British Columbia localities, down through the Puget Sound area to its finest development in the Willamette Valley and Douglas County, Oregon. It generally grows in the 20 to 40 inch rainfall areas, which include Portland. A tree that is as beautiful in the winter as in the summer, it has a spreading, rounded crown of gnarled branches. It can attain over 100 feet in height and 500 years in age. The largest Oregon white oak in the state is in Douglas County. In 1970 it measured nearly 23 feet in circumference and 98 feet in height. The mistletoe *Phoradendron flavescens* readily grows in the tree from Portland southward. The metropolitan area has several outstanding Oregon white oaks.

The Strong oak was planted in 1877 in front of the home of Curtis Clark Strong and his bride, Alice Henderson Strong (see photo). Mrs. Strong dug up a small sapling on the Henderson family farm near Amity, where she was born in 1852, and brought it to Portland. As her father drove the family buggy, she held the sapling between her knees for the long ride. In comparison with other local Oregon white oaks, the Strong oak is a slim model. It has suffered over the years from root pruning and careless car parking.

- 825 SE Miller St., 14'8" c, 4'8" d
- 619 N Winchell St., 14' c, 4'6" d
- 2137 SE 32nd Pl., 13'10" c, 4'5" d
- NW 23rd Ave. & Overton St., 13'6" c, 4'4" d

Quercus garryana, Oregon white or Garry oak. SW 29th & Sunset Blvd. 5-1-90. 15'2" c, 4'10" d. The classic shape. A beauty!

Quercus garryana. Oregon white or Garry oak. 1815 N Humboldt St. 5-19-90. 19'4" c, 6'2" d. It had to be measured below the start of its double trunk, thereby contributing to its enormous measurements.

Quercus palustris, Pin oak. 3664 SE Carlton St. 5-21-90. 11'7" c, 3'8" d.

Quercus palustris

(*kwer*-kus pa-*lus*-tris)

Pin oak
Deciduous

Native to central and eastern United States, pin oaks are scattered throughout Greater Portland. The leaves are distinctive: usually five-lobed, they are toothed and pointed. The leaf sinuses are U-shaped and extend nearly to the middle. Pin oak foliage turns an attractive red in the fall. This tree can reach a height of over 100 feet when mature. It is widely planted, both in the United States and in Europe, as a lawn and street tree, and needs a large expanse of lawn to set it off well.

- 4402 SW Shattuck Rd., 12'9" c, 4'1" d
- 3527 SE Ash St., 10'9" c, 3'5" d
- 8855 SW Canyon Ln., West Slope, 12' c, 3'10" d

Quercus rubra

(*kwer*-kus *rū*-bra)

Northern red oak
Deciduous

Quercus rubra, Northern red oak. 1961 SW Vista Ave. 4-25-90. 18' c, 5'9" d. Planted in the 1920s by Dr. A. S. Nichols. This tree may have a black oak in its lineage: its leaves and trunk are typical for a Northern red oak but its acorns resemble those of a black oak.

A fast-growing tree for big spaces, the red oak is native to the entire eastern half of the United States except for the Deep South. The leaves, which are a lustrous dark green in the summer, turn a beautiful red in the fall. They are relatively large with 7 to 11 pointed, toothed lobes separated by sinuses that extend halfway to the midrib. In the wild the tree can attain a height of over 150 feet, but it is more likely in the city to reach 75 feet with a spread of about two-thirds the height.

Northern red oaks and black oaks (*Quercus velutina*) share much of the same habitat and interbreed freely.

- 5700 SE Taylor St., 15' c, 4'9" d
- 1824 SE 23rd Ave., 11'6" c, 3'8" d (five in a row, planted by O. B. Stubbs around 1915)
- 10660 SE 21st St., Ledding Library, Milwaukie, 13'2" c, 4'2" d

Quercus rubra, Northern red oak. NE Pacific St. between Grand & 6th Aves. 10-30-90. 10' c, 3'2" d. Full fall foliage.

Rhododendron ponticum

(rō-dō-den-dron pon-ti-cum)

Ponticum rhododendron
Evergreen

Named for its place of origin—Pontus, an ancient country in what is now northeastern Turkey—this rhododendron is native to the Caucasus, Armenia, the Balkans, southern Spain, and Portugal. It is now naturalized in many parts of the British Isles. With an ultimate height of 30 feet, it becomes a small tree over time, especially if pruned to this shape. The leaves are dark green and shiny, and the flowers come in trusses of 10 to 15.

Many tiny ponticums were distributed at the 1905 Lewis & Clark Exposition in Portland. For reasons no one now knows, the ones that were left over were taken to Astoria and planted.

Rhododendron ponticum, Rhododendron. 1905 SE Larch Ave. 5-16-90. 4'4" c, 1'5" d. Since the house in the background was not built until 1911, it is doubtful the tree came from the Lewis & Clark Exposition of 1905. It is possible, however, that the tree was planted soon after the house was finished.

Robinia pseudoacacia

(rō-*bin*-i-a soo-dō-a-*kā*-sē-a)

Black locust
Deciduous

Robinia pseudoacacia, Black locust. 2235 & 2305 N Emerson St. 5-19-90. 12'9" c, 4'1" d. Massive specimens.

Native to the central and southern Appalachian Mountains, this tree escapes and naturalizes so that it can be found well outside its native range. In the Pacific Northwest it has become naturalized more extensively than any other tree, spreading by suckers and seed around abandoned farmsteads and river banks, almost appearing to be native. Although it can grow to 120 feet high, more usually it tops out at about 60 feet. The compound leaves have 7 to 19 leaflets, and the white flowers, borne in dense racemes, are extremely fragrant and last for over a week. As one might imagine, honeybees love this tree. Because black locust wood is resistant to decay, it has been used for centuries as fence posts and construction timber. The seeds, young leaves, and inner bark are all poisonous.

It is a tree easy to spot in May when it is in bloom. Greater Portland has several old black locusts. A close look at a blossom will show that the tree is a member of the pea family.

- NE 47th Ave. & Oregon St., 12' c, 3'10" d
- corner SW Macadam Rd. & Nebraska St., 10'5" c, 3'4" d

Salix babylonica

(sā-lix bab-i-*lon*-i-ka)

Weeping willow
Deciduous

The weeping willow came from China, but botanists now think that it is a plant of the past—that the true species is nowhere to be found. What we now call weeping willow is a hybrid, probably between *S. babylonica* and other willows. In any case, the tree has a short trunk, rounded crown, and long, pendulous branches that hang to the ground. The bark is gray and deeply furrowed.

Weeping willows are plentiful in the Portland area, especially near creeks, lakes, and marshes. Many in the Milwaukie area are related to an early Seth Lewelling tree cut down in 1940.

- SW Oleson Rd. on Fanno Creek
- 2125 NE Pacific St. (planted in the 1890s)

Salix babylonica, Weeping willow. 14019 N Gillihan Loop Rd., Sauvie Island. 4-12-90. 15'3" c, 4'10" d.

Salix matsudana 'Tortuosa'. Corkscrew willow. 2066 NW Kearney St. 2-28-91. 7'6" c, 2'5" d. As the leaves emerge, the contorted aspect of the tree is readily observable.

Salix matsudana 'Tortuosa'

(*sā*-lix mat-soo-*dā*-na tor-tū-*ō*-sa)

Corkscrew willow
Deciduous

Because of the twisting of this willow's contorted branches, the tree is a favorite of flower arrangers. It can reach 50 feet in height. The species is native to China and Korea, and the cultivar was introduced in the United States in 1923. There are many small and a few big corkscrew willows in the metropolitan area.

- 6217 SE 34th Ave.
- 6825 SW 63rd Ave., 9'2" c, 2'11" d
- 3749 N Melrose Dr.
- corner NE Knott St. & 19th Ave., 8'9" c, 2'9" d

Sassafras albidum

(*sas*-a-fras al-*bi*-dum)

Sassafras or Mitten tree
Deciduous

Sassafras albidum, Sassafras or Mitten tree. SW Upper Cascade Dr. (north side, near the top), Hoyt Arboretum. 11-3-90.

A native of the eastern United States from Massachusetts to South Carolina, this is a tree of strange structure. The leaves can be unlobed, two-lobed, or three-lobed with one lobe being large and the others small. The two-lobed leaves are shaped exactly like mittens, thus the reason for one of the common names. All parts of the tree are aromatic and yield oil much used in colonial times as a cure-all, but now banned by the government as unsafe. The fall color of the foliage is outstanding, varying from yellow to crimson all on one tree. The origin of the name *Sassafras* is obscure. Some think it derives from *saxifrage*, which means a rock-breaker, but the reason for this is unclear. Since its ultimate height is always less than 65 feet, it would fit well into a front or side yard. It should be more widely planted.

Sciadopytis verticillata

(sī-a-*dop*-it-is ver-ti-si-*lā*-ta)

Umbrella pine
Evergreen

Sciadopytis verticillata, Umbrella pine. 2870 NW Cornell Rd. 8-19-91. 4'3" c, 1'4" d. Planted around 1920 by Dr. Emil Ausplund, these two trimmed trees would be much taller if left to their own devices. During World War II, people asked the Ausplunds to cut the trees down because they were of Japanese origin!

Not a pine at all, this tree gets its common name from its leaves, which resemble the ribs of an umbrella. The tree belongs to the same family as redwoods and sequoias (Taxodiaceae). Very slow growing (not more than 6 inches a year when young), it can eventually attain a height of over 100 feet. Native to Japan, it is a handsome, full tree with deep green foliage that, because of its slow growth, makes a nice conifer addition to a small garden.

The Portland area has an amazing number of umbrella pines. Many are about the same size, suggesting that a nursery once had a large shipment.

- 406 NE Floral Pl.
- 288 SW Parkside Dr.
- 3711 SE Carlton St.
- NW 32nd & Thurman St. (two trees)
- 2104 NW Everett St.
- 1628 NE Thompson St. (two trees planted before 1910)
- 2370 SW Park Pl.

Sciadopytis verticillata, Umbrella pine. 10-2-90. Cone.

Sequoia sempervirens

(sē-*kwō*-ya sem-per-*vīr*-enz)

Coast redwood
Evergreen

Sequoia sempervirens, Coast redwood. 860 SW Vista Ave. 5-13-91. 20'5" c, 6'6" d. The largest redwood in Portland, this specimen was supposedly planted in the mid 1800s by a farmer named Jeffries. It was picked as Portland's favorite tree in 1987

The botanic name of the redwood is derived from Chief Sequoyah (1770–1843?), who invented the Cherokee alphabet. The Austrian botanist who named the tree gave no reason for having honored Chief Sequoyah. It was first discovered at Monterey, California, by a member of Malaspina's expedition of 1789–1794. The species name means always green, as, of course, this tree is unless it has suffered a severe winter (Portland's winter of 1990–1991 caused many redwood needles to turn brown). The needles are flat, short, and have a lacy effect. The cones are only an inch long. The fibrous bark is reddish brown, 3 to 10 inches thick. A common height for the redwood is 275 feet with a diameter of 10 feet, although this height is more often attained in the wild, where some trees reach 367 feet and a maximum age of about 2000 years. A native Oregon tree that grows as far north as the latitude of Brookings, the redwood thrives in its native coastal northern California. Heavily logged in the nineteenth and twentieth centuries, redwood now has several groups protecting its remaining tracts. There are many redwoods in the Portland area.

- 1415 SE Ramona St.
- 7112 N Richmond Ave.
- 2808 N Willamette Blvd., 11' c, 3'6" d
- X 1015 SE 17th Ave.
- 13720 SW Pacific Hwy., Tigard, 12'11" c, 4'1" d
- 5352 SE 37th Ave., 10'6" c, 3'4" d

Sequoiadendron giganteum

(sē-kwō-ya-*den*-dron jī-gan-*tē*-um)

Giant sequoia
Evergreen

Sequoiadendron giganteum, Giant sequoia. 2174 SW Laurel St. 7-1-91. 24′ c, 7′8″ d. This marvelous old tree was brought from California as a sapling by William Biddle Wells, who moved into his new house on Laurel St. about 1906. Other giant sequoias on Portland Heights were introduced by Colonel L. L. Hawkins in the early 1900s.

This species and *Sequoia sempervirens* are often confused because of their similar names, and, actually, the giant sequoia did not get its present botanic name until 1939. Both the foliage and the cones of the two species, however, are distinctly different in size and appearance. Although closely related botanically, their range is separate. All the giant sequoias in the Portland area are introduced. In their California habitat they may reach 3500 years in age and a height of up to 325 feet. In 1852 the northern-most grove in California (Calaveras) was discovered by a hunter employed to cater for workers in the 1849 goldrush. His mammoth "Discovery Tree" was measured at 100 feet in circumference. The tree, true to that era, became a challenge to the loggers, who determined to take it down and display the cross section. It resisted all attempts to fell it—even blasting—and finally toppled in a sharp breeze.

Recurrent fire is necessary to open the cones and release the seed for new trees. The tough bark protects the giant sequoias from fire, while younger and more-thin-skinned firs and pines are destroyed.

There are many giant sequoias in Greater Portland. Their pointy heads stick up above other trees, making them look like their tops had met up with a giant pencil sharpener, and so many are of a huge size to suggest that they were planted about the same time, perhaps from cones brought from California.

- 1225 SE 60th Ave., 25' c, 8' d
- 1728 SW Prospect Dr., 24' c, 7'8" d (planted 1910)
- 2238 SW Vista Ave., 23'2" c, 7'4" d
- 2188 SW Main St., 23' c, 7'4" d
- 14105 SE River Rd., Milwaukie, 23' c, 7'4" d
- 5810 SE Taylor St., 21'8" c, 6'11" d

Sequoiadendron giganteum, Giant sequoia. SE McLoughlin Blvd., Milwaukie. 2-23-91. Planted in 1937, this row of sequoias is gradually being destroyed to accommodate highway expansion. .

Sophora japonica

(sō-*fōr*-a ja-*pon*-i-ka)

Japanese pagoda or Chinese scholar tree
Deciduous

"Sophora" is an Arabian name for a tree with pea-shaped flowers. If the winter has not been too severe, this tree produces beautiful panicles of white-yellow flowers in late summer, and, in some years, also produces a spring bloom just as profuse. Capable of growing up to 80 feet in height, it generally does not reach this dimension in the city. It has a spreading habit with a rounded crown, and its leaves, which are lustrous green above and pale green beneath, are compound, as are the leaves of many trees in the pea family. Native to China and Korea, the pagoda tree is a handsome shade tree, and, because it blooms so late in the season, it can enhance the garden as well as the streetside.

Sophora japonica, Japanese pagoda tree or Chinese scholar tree. Corner NW 30th Ave. & Cornell Rd. 8-19-91. 7'5" c, 2'4" d. Felix Isherwood and his daughter Ruth drove to the outskirts of town in a horse and wagon to pick up this tree, which they planted around 1910.

Styrax japonicus

(*stī*-rax ja-*pon*-i-kus)

Japanese snowbell
Deciduous

Styrax japonicus, Japanese snowbell. 2988 SW Bennington Dr. 6-17-91.

An attractive tree that enhances the garden, the Japanese snowbell is small, never exceeding 50 feet in either height or width. In June its profuse and fragrant blossoms hang down from the branches on long stalks while the leaves extend upward from the top of the branches. In late summer and fall the fruit that forms continues to make the tree appealing. The Japanese snowbell is a native of China and Japan, and is found in many Portland gardens, although it is seldom visible from the street.

- 1520 SW Montgomery Dr.
- 15405 SE Wallace Rd., Oak Grove

Styrax japonicus, Japanese snowbell. 6-14-91. The blossoms.

Styrax japonicus, Japanese snowbell. 10-2-90. The seeds.

Tamarix parviflora

Tamarix parviflora, Tamarisk. 2705 NE Halsey St. 4-23-90.

(*tam*-a-rix par-vi-*flōr*-a)

Tamarisk
Deciduous

Although this small tree has a history of confusing taxonomists, its present species name is now widely accepted. It is spring-flowering, with pink, profuse blossoms that appear before the leaves and last several weeks. While it never exceeds 30 feet in height, it can get quite wide. A native of southeastern Europe, it is a hardy tree, thriving in poor soil conditions. A drive around the metropolitan area in late April and May will put many tamarisks in view. If they look unhealthy, they may have received too much fertilizer.

- X 415 SE 35th Ave.
- 7074 SE Division St.
- 2615 SE 43rd Ave.
- 1405 SE Tacoma St.

Taxus brevifolia

(*tax*-us bre-vi-*fō*-li-a)

Western yew
Evergreen

Very few Western yews grow along Greater Portland streets. In the early 1990s this species became sought after for its bark, found to help in some cancer therapy. Almost immediately bark thieves began to indiscriminately kill yews for this precious commodity, both in the wild and in urban areas. To protect this tree from death by the hand of bark peelers, we have chosen to provide neither photograph nor addresses.

Thuja plicata, Western redcedar or Giant arborvitae.
21440 SE Stark St. 5-1-91. 11' c, 3'6" d. This grove of
Western redcedars once was part of a nursery.

Thuja plicata

(*thew*-ya pli-*kā*-ta)

Western redcedar
or Giant arborvitae
Evergreen

A Pacific Northwest native, this beauty is capable of attaining over 250 feet in height and 20 feet in diameter in the wild. The largest known Western redcedars are estimated to be about 1000 years old. In the city this tree reaches well over 70 feet. A row of them is often used as a high hedge or windbreak. Pacific Northwest Native Americans used this tree for everything from diapers made from the bark to canoes burned and carved out of the entire trunk.

The Western redcedar has lustrous green foliage and lighter green new growth. The bark is reddish, thick, and fibrous. The cones are small and, when old, resemble tiny, dried brown flowers. The tree is highly prized by the timber industry, so very few virgin stands are left.

Although the tree is characteristic of moist areas and reaches optimum development where the rainfall exceeds that of Portland, the city area abounds in young Western redcedars. Old trees grow in Forest Park and the Hoyt Arboretum, away from the street. From a distance it is sometimes difficult to tell the Western redcedar apart from the Port Orford cedar, the Alaska cedar, and the giant sequoia.

In Gresham, along SE Hogan Avenue just south of Palmquist Road and stretching to the city limits, is a collection of Hogan cedar trees. No one knows for sure how this tall variety of Western redcedar with a very slender, conical shape got to this approximately one-square-mile area. Thought not to be indigenous, some people believe the Hogan cedar was brought in by a Chinese nursery owner, while others hypothesize that early Dant and Russell lumber merchants, who established the Ambleside Corporation in this vicinity, brought it in. The first description of it occurred in 1913. Now this variety can be found in many spots in northwest Oregon—from cabins near Mount Hood to gardens near Corbett and beyond. It is interesting that the seeds breed true.

- 8th St. between A & B Aves., Lake Oswego, 12' c, 3'10'' d (four trees)
- 2605 SE 33rd Ave., 10'7'' c, 3'4'' d
- SE 28th Ave. near Carlton St., Eastmoreland Golf Course (a variegated form, row of 25)

Thuja plicata, Western redcedar or Giant arborvitae. 7754 SE Milwaukie Ave. 6-29-91. Two variegated cultivars.

Tilia platyphyllos

(*til*-i-a plat-i-*fil*-us)

Bigleaf linden
Deciduous

The bigleaf linden, which grows to 80 feet and higher, is a European native that has been planted there as an ornamental for centuries. The tree has a distinctive leaf, about 2 to 5 inches long (not really very big), shaped much like a heart with a regular serrate edge. It flowers in the typical linden way: a cyme grows out of a long narrow bract coming out of the branch at the same place as the leaf stalk, each cyme usually bearing four to five yellow flowers. It is the earliest (May or early June) flowering of all the lindens, much to the delight of honeybees. Many of Portland's parks have these lindens, and several streets in Sellwood are lined with them. They form extended allées at the Fountainbleu gardens in France.

- 3712 SE Carlton St., 7'2" c, 2'3" d
- X 3354 SE Kelly St., 7' c, 2'3" d

Tilia platyphyllos, Bigleaf linden. SE Reed College Pl. 5-21-90. A most attractive allée.

Tilia tomentosa, Silver linden. Peninsula Park, stretching between N Albina & Kerby Sts. 5-19-90. Taken on a windy day. Planted in 1909.

Tilia tomentosa

(*til*-i-a tō-men-*tō*-sa)

Silver linden
Deciduous

A good shade tree, the silver linden can eventually reach over 100 feet in height. The leaf color is outstanding: the top is a lustrous, glistening dark green, and the bottom is silvery with short, thick "fur" beneath. When the wind blows these changing surfaces create a pleasing effect. Generally the last of the lindens to flower, the silver linden does so in typical linden fashion (cf. bigleaf linden). The yellow flowers are said to be narcotic to honeybees. The silver linden makes an excellent street tree as it is tolerant of heat and drought. Not many of of this species grow in the Greater Portland area.

- 2715 SE 33rd Ave., 9'9" c, 3'1" d
- between NE 10th & 11th Aves. & Brazee St., 10'2" c, 3'3" d (row of four, planted before 1910)
- 2870 NW Cornell Rd., 7'7" c, 2'5" d (planted by Dr. Emil Ausplund around 1920)
- 15490 SE Wallace Rd., Oak Grove

Tilia sp. 7-8-91. All linden blooms are similar. Each species has its own blooming period.

Trachycarpus fortunei, Chinese windmill palm. 1834 SE 22nd Ave. 6-27-91.

Trachycarpus fortunei

(trāk-ē-*kar*-pus for-*tū*-nē-ī)

Chinese windmill palm
Evergreen

This hardy palm comes from central and southern China and can be found in gardens as far north as Vancouver, British Columbia, where the moderate maritime climate helps it survive. Males and females are separate trees. A single, shaggy, fibrous trunk can reach over 30 feet in height. The fanlike leaves, up to 3 feet wide, are clustered at the top. The Portland area has just a few of these palms, which seem to make it through the winter (even the harsh one of 1990–1991), but do not look happy.

- 2525 NE Glisan St.
- 40 N State St., Lake Oswego
- 80 SW Murray Rd, Beaverton
- 1616 SE 30th Ave.

Tsuga heterophylla, Western hemlock. 455 SE 68th Ave. 12-2-89. 10'8" c, 3'5" d.

Tsuga heterophylla

(*soo*-ga het-er-ō-*fil*-a)

Western hemlock
Evergreen

Washington's state tree, this conifer can be spotted from afar by its drooping leader. The new growth at the top hangs over as though a weight were affixed to the end. The coastal Northwest is home to this tree, from south central Alaska to northern California, but it also occurs in wet places in the Rockies of northwestern Montana. The needles are small, flat, blunt, and of unequal length, but always rather short. The species name means "variable leaves." The fine foliage gives the tree a delicate look. The cones are also small—less than an inch long—and profuse both on the tree and on the ground around it. The tree can reach over 200 feet in height and a maximum age of about 500 years. Not many large Western hemlocks are in the Portland area near the street.

- SW Cascade Dr., south of parking lot, Hoyt Arboretum, 10' c, 3'2" d
- 3226 SE Division St., 8'2" c, 2'7" d
- 2307 NE Everett St., 8' c, 2'7" d
- SE 39th Ave. & Glisan St., Coe Circle
- SW Council Crest Dr. & Patrick Pl. (two trees)
- 1837 SE 22nd Ave.

Ulmus americana

(*ul*-mus a-mer-i-*kā*-na)

American elm
Deciduous

Ulmus americana, American elm. Clackamette Dr. near SE McLoughlin Blvd. & I-205. 5-4-91, 15'2" c, 4'10" d. George Abernethy, provisional governor of Oregon, planted this elm in 1846 at the northeast side of his house. Although the house is long gone, the Abernethy Elm remains. It has survived a number of floods.

For hundreds of years the American elm was the most widely planted street tree in America: its form is beautiful, its foliage luxuriant, and it is relatively unmessy. The tallest known elm tree in the country grows in Tennessee; it is 160 feet high. Unfortunately, the American elm is highly susceptible to Dutch elm disease (first noted in Holland about 1919), so although its native habitat extends from Newfoundland to Florida and west to the foot of the Rockies, the East and the Midwest have lost nearly all their elms. As of winter, 1992, Portland has lost about 87 trees to the disease, the first case having appeared in 1977. In June, 1991, the city began prophylactic treatment of Portland's downtown Park Block elms against this disease— costly but worth it. Think what downtown Portland would look like without its elms!

It is estimated that the Portland area has about 5500 elms (both American elms and European elms). Many, like those in the Park Blocks, were planted last century. Several of Portland's older neighborhoods have street after street lined with these trees.

- corner SW 21st Ave. & Montgomery Dr., 14'6" c, 4'7" d
- 560 1st St., Lake Oswego, 13'9" c, 4'5" d
- 1150 SW King Ave., 13'5" c, 4'3" d
- 1924 SE Umatilla St., 12' c, 3'10" d

Ulmus americana, American elm. SW Rose Garden Blvd., Washington Park. 9-13-90. 11'4" c, 3'7" d. Planted in 1932 by the Daughters of the American Revolution, the Washington Elm is a descendent of the tree under which George Washington took command of the colonial army.

Ulmus americana, American elm. SW 10th Ave. near Jefferson St. 7-18-91. 11'8" c, 3'9" d. The Burrell Elm, the second historic tree recognized by the city, was planted in 1870 at the house of Martin S. and Rosetta Frazar Burrell, which stood on 10th Ave. where the YWCA is today. Burrell, who died in 1903, came from Sheffield, Ohio, in 1856, and ran a farm implement business. His wife, an early philanthropist, established the First Unitarian Church.

Ulmus americana, American elm. 2424 SW Montgomery Dr. 5-20-90. 11'11" c, 3'10" d. A classic specimen. Planted in 1918.

Ulmus glabra

(*ul*-mus *gla*-bra)

Scotch or Wych elm
Deciduous

Ulmus glabra, Scotch or Wych elm. 6125 SW Boundary St. 7-20-91. 13'5" c, 4'3" d.

The Scotch elm is a massive tree, reaching 100 feet in height and nearly that size in crown spread. The leaves on top are a darker green than the green of other elms, but underneath they are contrastingly light, and they are rough to the touch. In the early summer the leaves are a favorite diet of tiny black worms, who eventually create a lacy look by eating everything except the veins. In heavy worm years the tree suffers because of a lack of photosynthetic material. Native to north and central Europe and Asia Minor, this species has been cultivated since antiquity.

- X 2752 NW Upshur St., 13'2" c, 4'2" d
- SW 14th Ave. in front of Lincoln High School, 11'9" c, 3'9" d
- 239 NW Skyline Blvd., 13'3" c, 4'3" d

Ulmus parvifolia

(*ul*-mus par-vi-*fōl*-i-a)

Chinese elm
Deciduous

This native of China, Korea, and Japan has a broad, rounded crown of spreading branches. With smaller leaves than most of the other elms, this elm is one of the few to both flower and form seeds in the fall. Seldom reaching over 50 feet in height, it retains its leaves all winter in warm climates. Considered an attractive tree, it will fit into a smaller garden because of its size. Brooklyn Park has several of these trees around the periphery.

Ulmus parvifolia, Chinese elm. SE Milwaukie Ave. & Haig St., Brooklyn Park. 6-29-91. 9'7" c, 3'1" d.

Ulmus procera

(*ul*-mus prō-*sēr*-a)

English elm
Deciduous

Ulmus procera 'Argenteo-variegata', Variegated English elm. 2433 SE Grant St. 5-21-91. 10'3" c, 3'3" d. This form is rare in the Portland area.

A European elm, native from England to central and south Europe, this big but lacy-looking tree can reach a height of about 150 feet. The crown is typically dense but irregular and the smaller branches may have corky wings. The leaves of this elm are smaller than those of the American elm. The species is a popular tree in the northeast United States. It was lumber from this tree that brought the elm bark beetle, carrying Dutch elm disease, to the United States in 1930.

- 2455 NW Johnson St., 12' c, 3'10" d
- 2363 NW Flanders St., 12'8" c, 4' d
- SE 58th Ave. & Scholls Ferry Rd. (Sylvan interchange), 12'8" c, 4' d

Ulmus × *vegeta* 'Camperdownii', Camperdown elm. McLoughlin Ave. exit, at east end of Ross Island bridge. 4-15-90. It is difficult to believe that this enormous specimen, with boughs cascading many feet over a wall, is actually a tree. The Poulsen house stands in the background.

Ulmus × *vegeta* 'Camperdownii'

(*ul*-mus ve-*jē*-ta cam-per-*down*-ē-ī)

Camperdown elm
Deciduous

The botanic name of this tree seems to constantly change. Be that as it may, the tree originated as a seedling about 150 years ago and was discovered creeping along the ground at Camperdown House near Dundee, Scotland. It is grafted onto other elm stock at about 7 feet to give it a start off the ground.

Portland's most spectacular specimen can be seen on the McLoughlin Blvd. exit at the east end of the Ross Island Bridge (see photo).

- 1106 SE Lambert St.
- 1505 SE Miller St.
- 35 SE Laurelhurst Pl.
- 5432 SE Hawthorne St.

Umbellularia californica, California laurel or Oregon
Myrtle. 1903 SE Ankeny St. 3-15-91. 10'8" c, 3'5" d.

Umbellularia californica

(um-bel-ū-*lar*-i-a kal-i-*fōr*-ni-ka)

California laurel
or Oregon myrtle
Evergreen

As the common names indicate, this broadleaf evergreen is a native of
Oregon and California. It grows naturally only in southwest Oregon,
but can be found in the California coast range and lower elevations of
the Sierra Nevada. It can attain a height of 175 feet and a width of 100
feet in the wild. The girth of the largest California laurel in Oregon,
located in the Siskiyou National Forest, measured 41'9" in 1978. The
leaves of the California laurel have a powerful aroma and have been
used sometimes, in a small portion, to substitute in cooking for the
European bay leaf (*Laurus nobilis*). The tree is slow growing. In the fall
it produces a marble-sized, dark blue fruit loved by the birds. Several
large California laurels can be found in Greater Portland.

- between SE 21st & 22nd Aves. on Bybee Blvd.
- 1350 SE Flavel St.
- SW Viewpoint Terr. & Bancroft St.
- 7545 N Kerby Ave.
- 3235 SE Harrison St., Milwaukie
- 2411 SE Tamarack Ave., 11'10" c, 3'9" d

Zelkova serrata, Japanese zelkova. SE Oak Ct. & 41st Ave. 7-1-91. 8'9" c, 2'9" d. Actually two trees planted way too close together in the early 1940s.

Zelkova serrata

(zel-*kō*-va ser-*rā*-ta)

Japanese zelkova
Deciduous

This native of Japan is a member of the elm family. It has graceful symmetry and ascending branches, and is relatively resistant to Dutch elm disease. The leaves turn red in the fall, and the bark on older trees is a characteristic brown, mottled and flaky. The tree yields hard, pliable wood widely used in Japan for building purposes and furniture. Although it makes a good street tree, since its ultimate height is about 130 feet it should not be planted under telephone wires.

- SW Cascade Dr. & Upper Cascade Dr., Hoyt Arboretum (a grove of 11 trees)
- O'Bryant Square—SW Park Ave., Washington St., 9th Ave. & Stark St. (11 trees on the periphery)
- corner SW King Ave. & Park Pl.

Best Tree Viewing Times

The times given are only approximate and, depending on the weather—a cold winter, an early spring, or a dry summer, for example—may vary up to three weeks in either direction. Many species are listed more than once because they have more than one "best" viewing time.

All year round

Abies concolor (White fir)
Abies grandis (Grand fir)
Abies pinsapo (Spanish fir)
Abies procera (Noble fir)
Araucaria araucana (Monkey puzzle)
Arbutus menziesii (Pacific madrone)
Calocedrus decurrens (Incense cedar)
Catalpa bignonoides (Southern catalpa)
Cedrus atlantica (Atlas cedar)
Cedrus deodara (Deodar)
Cedrus libani (Cedar of Lebanon)
Chamaecyparis lawsoniana (Port Orford cedar)
Chamaecyparis nootkatensis (Alaska cedar)
Cryptomeria japonica (Cryptomeria)
Cunninghamia lanceolata (China fir)
Eriobotrya japonica (Loquat)
Magnolia grandiflora (Southern magnolia)
Picea abies (Norway spruce)
Picea breweriana (Brewer spruce)
Picea pungens (Colorado spruce)

Picea sitchensis (Sitka spruce)
Pinus contorta (Lodgepole pine)
Pinus coulteri (Coulter pine)
Pinus densiflora (Japanese red pine)
Pinus monticola (Western white pine)
Pinus nigra (Austrian pine)
Pinus ponderosa (Ponderosa pine)
Pseudotsuga menziesii (Douglas fir)
Quercus garryana (Oregon white oak)
Sciadopytis verticillata (Umbrella pine)
Sequoia sempervirens (Coast redwood)
Sequoiadendron giganteum (Giant sequoia)
Thuja plicata (Western redcedar)
Trachycarpus fortunei (Chinese windmill palm)
Tsuga heterophylla (Western hemlock)
Umbellularia californica (California laurel)

March

Acer platanoides (Norway maple)
Acer pseudoplatanus (Sycamore maple)
Acer rubrum (Red maple)
Acer saccharinum (Silver maple)
Larix decidua (European larch)
Larix kaempferi (Japanese larch)
Larix occidentalis (Western larch)
Magnolia dawsoniana (Dawson's magnolia)
Magnolia denudata (Yulan magnolia)
Magnolia sargentiana var. *robusta* (Sargent magnolia)
    —perhaps late February
Magnolia × *soulangiana* (Saucer magnolia)
Malus floribunda (Japanese flowering crabapple)
Prunus avium 'Royal Ann' (Royal Ann cherry)
Prunus domestica (Plum)
Prunus serrulata (Japanese flowering cherry)
Prunus subhirtella 'Pendula' (Weeping Japanese cherry)
Pyrus calleryana (Callery pear)
Pyrus communis (Pear)
Salix babylonica (Weeping willow)
Salix matsudana 'Tortuosa' (Corkscrew willow)

April

Acer macrophyllum (Bigleaf maple)
Acer palmatum (Japanese maple)
Aesculus hippocastanum (Common horsechestnut)
Aesculus × *carnea* (Red horsechestnut)
Arbutus menziesii (Pacific madrone)
Betula nigra (River birch)
Betula papyrifera (Paper birch)
Betula pendula (European white birch)
Cercis canadensis (Eastern redbud)
Cornus florida (Flowering dogwood)
Cornus nuttallii (Pacific dogwood)
Crataegus laevigata (English hawthorn)
Crataegus × *lavallei* (Lavalle hawthorne)
Davidia involucrata (Dove tree)
Ginkgo biloba (Ginkgo)
Gleditsia triacanthos var. *inermis* (Thornless common honeylocust)
Koelreuteria paniculata (Golden rain tree)
Laburnum anagyroides (Goldenchain tree)
Metasequoia glyptostroboides (Dawn redwood)
Paulownia tomentosa (Empress tree)
Photinia serrulata (Chinese photinia)
Prunus avium (Sweet cherry)
Prunus serrulata 'Kwanzan' (Japanese flowering cherry)
Tamarix parviflora (Tamarisk)

May

Acer campestre (Hedge maple)
Acer negundo 'Variegatum' (Ghost tree)
Aesculus octandra (Yellow buckeye)
Cercidiphyllum japonicum (Katsura tree)
Cladrastis lutea (Yellowwood)
Fagus sylvatica (European beech)
Juglans nigra (Black walnut)
Juglans regia (English walnut)
Liriodendron tulipifera (Tulip tree)
Magnolia acuminata (Cucumber tree)
Platanus occidentalis (American planetree)

Platanus × *acerifolia* (London planetree)
Populus × *canadensis* (Carolina poplar)
Quercus bicolor (Swamp white oak)
Quercus garryana (Oregon white oak)
Quercus palustris (Pin oak)
Quercus rubra (Northern red oak)
Rhododendron ponticum (Rhododendron)
Robinia pseudoacacia (Black locust)
Tilia platyphyllos (Bigleaf linden)
Tilia tomentosa (Silver linden)
Ulmus americana (American elm)
Ulmus parvifolia (Chinese elm)
Ulmus procera (English elm)
Zelkova serrata (Japanese zelkova)

June

Almost all deciduous trees are in full leaf by the end of June, and, because their leaves are fresh, this is a good month to view them.

Carpinus betulus (European hornbeam)
Carpinus caroliniana (American hornbeam)
Catalpa speciosa (Northern catalpa)
Magnolia tripetala (Umbrella magnolia)
Styrax japonicus (Japanese snowbell)

July

Ailanthus altissima (Tree of heaven)
Albizia julibrissin (Silk tree)
Castanea dentata (American chestnut)
Castanea sativa (Spanish chestnut)
Catalpa bignonoides (Southern catalpa)
Clerodendrum trichotomum (Glory bower)
Fraxinus latifolia (Oregon ash)
Koelreuteria paniculata (Golden rain tree)
Magnolia grandiflora (Southern magnolia)
Sophora japonica (Japanese pagoda tree)

August

Ailanthus altissima (Tree of heaven)
Albizia julibrissin (Silk tree)
Carya ovata (Shagbark hickory)
Carya tomentosa (Mockernut hickory)
Clerodendrum trichotomum (Glory bower)
Hydrangea paniculata (Panicle hydrangea)
Laegerstroemia indica (Crapemyrtle)
Magnolia grandiflora (Southern magnolia)
Sophora japonica (Japanese pagoda tree)

Fall (late September, October, or November)

Acer macrophyllum (Bigleaf maple)
Acer palmatum (Japanese maple)
Acer platanoides (Norway maple)
Acer rubrum (Red maple)
Acer saccharum (Sugar maple)
Aesculus glabra (Ohio buckeye)
Aesculus octandra (Yellow buckeye)
Arbutus menziesii (Pacific madrone)
Betula nigra (River birch)
Betula papyrifera (Paper birch)
Betula pendula (European white birch)
Cercidiphyllum japonicum (Katsura tree)
Clerodendrum trichotomum (Glory bower)
Cornus florida (Flowering dogwood)
Cornus nuttallii (Pacific dogwood)
Crataegus × lavallei (Lavalle hawthorn)
Diospyros kaki (Japanese persimmon)
Fraxinus latifolia (Oregon ash)
Ginkgo biloba (Ginkgo)
Hydrangea paniculata (Panicle hydrangea)
Koelreuteria paniculata (Golden rain tree)
Larix decidua (European larch)
Larix kaempferi (Japanese larch)
Larix occidentalis (Western larch)
Liquidambar styraciflua (American sweetgum)
Liriodendrum tulipifera (Tulip tree)
Metasequoia glyptostroboides (Dawn redwood)
Nyssa sylvatica (Tupelo)

Oxydendrum arboreum (Sourwood)
Populus nigra 'Italica' (Lombardy poplar)
Populus tremuloides (Quaking aspen)
Populus trichocarpa (Black cottonwood)
Populus × *canadensis* (Carolina poplar)
Pyrus calleryana (Callery pear)
Pyrus communis (Pear)
Quercus palustris (Pin oak)
Quercus rubra (Northern red oak)
Sassafras albidum (Sassafras)
Styrax japonicus (Japanese snowbell)
Zelkova serrata (Japanese zelkova)

Winter

Eriobotrya japonica (Loquat)

Nine Tree Tours

Though notable trees are scattered throughout Greater Portland, we have selected nine neighborhoods in which a good collection of trees can be seen in a relatively small area. Seven of the tours are designed for pedestrians, two for motorists and bicyclists.

Each walk has a map with numbers that correspond to the accompanying list of trees; the starting point is circled. While we have placed these numbers on the maps as accurately as possible in such limited space, when you get out on the street you may at times wonder which tree is designated. Referring to the photograph of the species in the text will often help you make a decision. (An asterisk beside a tree name indicates that a photograph of this very tree appears in the main part of the book; a number beside a tree name indicates how many examples of that species are found at the identified location.)

Not every tree along a route is identified. Some, but by no means all, the species are described in this book. Most of the time we point out a species only once per route, assuming that you will be able to spot it again when and if it occurs. In cases where we mention a species more than once, we believe the particular trees are worth noting. Often elms are designated simply as "European." Because we could not reach the leaves, flowers, or seeds of these trees to verify the species, we could only distinguish New World elms (*Ulmus americana*) from Old World elms (*Ulmus* spp.).

We trust you will enjoy these walks and drives as much as we have. As you become familiar with the trees in these nine neighborhoods, we also trust you will learn to identify the notable trees in your own neighborhood.

Irvington

This neighborhood is named for William Irving, a captain and ship owner who came to Oregon in 1849 and claimed a square mile. Nine years later he sold his interests and moved away. His heirs platted Irvington in 1887, and, following the Lewis & Clark Exposition of 1905, the area filled in rapidly.

1 Common horsechestnut (*Aesculus hippocastanum*) row of 7
2 Caucasian wingnut (*Pterocarya fraxinifolia*) row of 7
3 American sycamore (*Platanus occidentalis*) row of 8
4 Sycamore maple (*Acer pseudoplatanus*) row of 4
5 Norway maple (*Acer platanoides*) 3
6 English elm (*Ulmus procera*)
7 Port Orford cedar (*Chamaecyparis lawsoniana*)
8 Deodar (*Cedrus deodara*) 2
9 Monkey puzzle (*Araucaria araucana*) female; cut down April 1992
10 Purple beech (*Fagus sylvatica* 'Atropunicea') *
11 Colorado blue spruce (*Picea pungens*)
12 Saucer magnolia (*Magnolia* × *soulangiana*)
13 Smooth leaf elm (*Ulmus carpinifolia*)
14 Common horsechestnut (*Aesculus hippocastanum*) row of 5
15 Bigleaf maple (*Acer macrophyllum*)
16 Western redcedar (*Thuja plicata*)
17 Sugar maple (*Acer saccharum*) 2
18 London planetree (*Platanus* × *acerifolia*) 2
19 Pissard's plum (*Prunus cerasifera* 'Atropurpurea')

20 Tulip tree (*Liriodendron tulipifera*)
21 Silk tree (*Albizia julibrissin*)
22 Silver maple (*Acer saccharinum*) 2
23 Bigleaf maple (*Acer macrophyllum*)
24 Black walnut (*Juglans nigra*)
25 Bigleaf maple (*Acer macrophyllum*) row of 5
26 Monkey puzzle (*Araucaria araucana*) male
27 English oak (*Quercus robur*)
28 Pin oak (*Quercus palustris*) 2
29 Southern magnolia (*Magnolia grandiflora*)
30 Ghost tree (*Acer negundo* 'Variegatum')
31 Saucer magnolia (*Magnolia* × *soulangiana*)
32 Tulip tree (*Liriodendron tulipifera*) 3
33 Umbrella pine (*Sciadopytis verticillata*) 2
34 English walnut (*Juglans regia*)
35 Leyland cypress (× *Cupressocyparis leylandii*)
36 Ginkgo (*Ginkgo biloba*) corner of 8
37 Dawn redwood (*Metasequoia glyptostroboides*)
38 Coast redwood (*Sequoia sempervirens*) 2
39 European white birch (*Betula pendula* 'Dalecarlica') 3
40 American sweetgum (*Liquidambar styraciflua*) 2 *

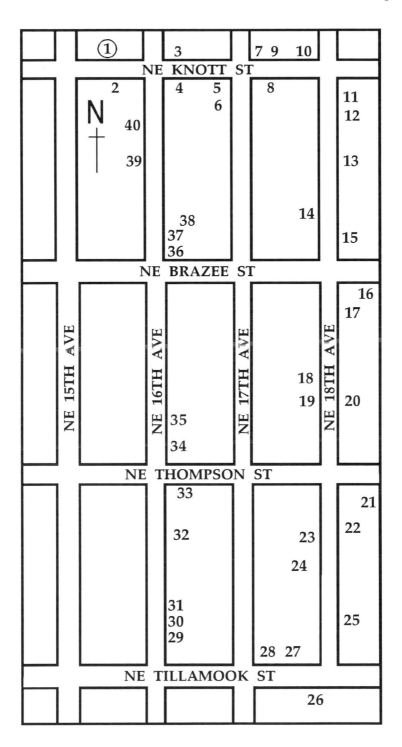

Mount Tabor

At the dawning of the twentieth century, the west slope of Mount Tabor was the site of several nurseries and orchards. Henry Prettyman, whose father had a 640-acre land claim in the area in 1848, stocked a large nursery on Baseline (Stark Street) with 200,000 trees. John Broetje, who later relocated to Oak Grove where he planted giant sequoias around his home, owned a nursery at the head of Asylum Road (Hawthorne Street), where Dr. Hawthorne ran an asylum, and Prettyman Avenue (55th Avenue). When street cars reached Mount Tabor in 1889, denser development followed. Several houses in the neighborhood date to the 1890s and a few to the 1880s. There are many fine gardens and tree specimens.

1 Yellowwood (*Cladrastis lutea*)
2 Western hemlock (*Tsuga heterophylla*) hedge
3 Western redcedar (*Thuja plicata*)
4 Japanese maple (*Acer palmatum*)
5 Deodar (*Cedrus deodara*)
6 Tulip tree (*Liriodendron tulipifera*) row of 4
7 Black locust (*Robinia pseudoacacia*)
8 California laurel (*Umbellularia californica*)
9 Pacific dogwood (*Cornus nuttallii*)
10 Austrian pine (*Pinus nigra*)
11 Incense cedar (*Calocedrus decurrens*)
12 Sitka spruce (*Picea sitchensis*)
13 Port Orford cedar (*Chamaecyparis lawsoniana*) 3
14 Northern red oak (*Quercus rubra*)
15 Vine maple (*Acer circinatum*)
16 English walnut (*Juglans regia*)
17 Silver maple (*Acer saccharinum*)
18 Lodgepole pine (*Pinus contorta*)
19 Alaska cedar (*Chamaecyparis nootkatensis*)
20 Shagbark hickory (*Carya ovata*)
21 Giant sequoia (*Sequoiadendron giganteum*)
22 Coast redwood (*Sequoia sempervirens*)
23 Silk tree (*Albizia julibrissin*)
24 Bigleaf maple (*Acer macrophyllum*) 2
25 European white birch (*Betula pendula*) row of 4
26 Norway maple (*Acer platanoides*) row of 4
27 Pin oak (*Quercus palustris*)
28 Tamarisk (*Tamarix parviflora*)
29 Black locust (*Robinia pseudoacacia*)
30 Douglas fir (*Pseudotsuga menziesii*)
31 Giant sequoia (*Sequoiadendron giganteum*)
32 Pacific madrone (*Arbutus menziesii*)
33 Sycamore maple (*Acer pseudoplatanus*) 3
34 Ponderosa pine (*Pinus ponderosa*)
35 Hedge maple (*Acer campestre*)
36 Northern catalpa (*Catalpa speciosa*) row of 5

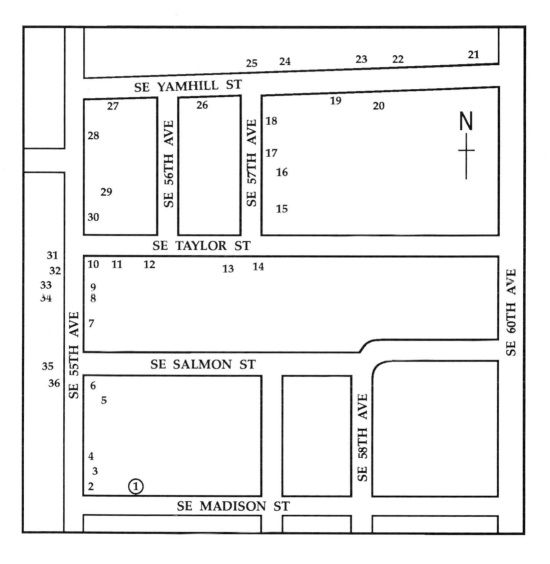

Oak Grove

for bicyclists and motorists

Originally called Territorial Road, River Road is bordered by many trees planted when Charles and Jacob Risley owned this land. Oatfield Road, originally a dirt track bordered by oaks and Douglas firs, ran through the 600 acres of farm and orchards owned by Michael Oatfield. John Broetje, who planted giant sequoias throughout the area, some in front of two Oatfield homes, operated a fine nursery on Courtney Avenue with his son Julius. Another son, John, remained on the family property, where he developed vineyards.

Begin at SE River Road where it intersects SE Jennings Avenue. Set your odometer to 0 and travel north on River Road.

Miles	Side	Tree
0.05	R	Coast redwood (*Sequoia sempervirens*)
0.05	L	Sitka spruce (*Picea sitchensis*)
0.1	L	Ponderosa pine (*Pinus ponderosa*)
0.1	R	Douglas fir (*Pseudotsuga menziesii*)
0.1	L	Bigleaf linden (*Tilia platyphyllos*)
0.4	R	Blue Atlas cedar (*Cedrus atlantica* 'Glauca')
0.5	R	Black walnut (*Juglans nigra*) 3
0.6	R	Black walnut (*Juglans nigra*)
0.65	R	Giant sequoia (*Sequoiadendron giganteum*)
0.7	R	European elm (*Ulmus* sp.)
0.8	R	Eastern redbud (*Cercis canadensis*)
1.0	R	Eastern white pine (*Pinus strobus*)

Miles	Side	Tree
1.0	L	Northern catalpa (*Catalpa speciosa*)
1.0	R	Port Orford cedar (*Chamaecyparis lawsoniana*)
1.0	R	Noble fir (*Abies procera*)
1.2	R	Grand fir (*Abies grandis*)
1.3	R	Oregon white oak (*Quercus garryana*) 2
1.4	R	Empress tree (*Paulownia tomentosa*)
1.5	R	Giant sequoia (*Sequoiadendron giganteum*)
2.0	L	Sassafras (*Sassafras albidum*) 2
2.5	R	Deodar (*Cedrus deodara*) 2
2.5	R	Persimmon (*Diospyros* sp.)
2.6	R	Dawn redwood (*Metasequoia glyptostroboides*)
2.7	L	Giant sequoia (*Sequoiadendron giganteum*)
2.9	R	Spanish chestnut (*Castanea sativa*)
3.35	L	Silk tree (*Albizia julibrissin*)

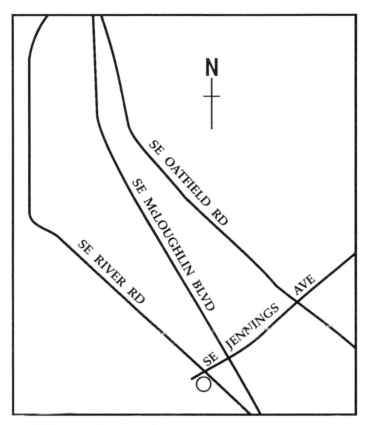

Return to SE Jennings Avenue where it intersects Oatfield Road. Set your odometer to 0 and travel north on Oatfield.

Miles	Side	Tree
0.0	L	Oregon white oak (*Quercus garryana*)
0.4	L	Northern catalpa (*Catalpa speciosa*) 14
1.0	L	Ponderosa pine (*Pinus ponderosa*)
1.1	R	Colorado spruce (*Picea pungens*)
1.2	L	Atlas cedar (*Cedrus atlantica*)
1.25	R	Scarlet oak (*Quercus coccinea*)
1.3	R	Bur oak (*Quercus macrocarpa*)
1.35	R	Lady apple (*Malus* sp.)
1.5	R	Colorado spruce (*Picea pungens*) 2

Miles	Side	Tree
1.6	R	Engelmann spruce (*Picea engelmannii*)
1.6	R	Giant sequoia (*Sequoiadendron giganteum*) grove of 17
1.8	R	
2.2	L&R	
2.4	L	White fir (*Abies concolor*)
2.5	R	California juniper (*Juniperus californica*)
2.7	L	Atlas cedar (*Cedrus atlantica*)
2.7	L	Deodar (*Cedrus deodara*)
3.2	L	Coast redwood (*Sequoia sempervirens*) 2
3.3	R	Ponderosa pine (*Pinus ponderosa*)

Portland Heights

This neighborhood was at first an area of summer retreats and small farms. When made accessible by cable car in 1898, development accelerated, lots were laid out, and, with the advent of streetcars, the neighborhood's popularity as a gracious urban area grew. Improved streets were bordered with fine trees, which, today, are lovely, big specimens. This is an easy walk with several notable trees.

1 Norway spruce (*Picea abies*) *
2 White fir (*Abies concolor*) *
3 Giant sequoia (*Sequoiadendron giganteum*) *
4 European elm (*Ulmus* sp.)
5 Oregon ash (*Fraxinus latifolia*) *
6 Silver maple (*Acer saccharinum*) corner of 4
7 Norway spruce (*Picea abies*) 2
8 Incense cedar (*Calocedrus decurrens*)
9 European elm (*Ulmus* sp.) 2
10 European white birch (*Betula pendula*) row of 4
11 English elm (*Ulmus procera*) row of 5
12 English elm (*Ulmus procera*) row of 5
13 Northern red oak (*Quercus rubra*) *
14 Lombardy poplar (*Populus nigra* 'Italica') row of 5
15 Cedar of Lebanon (*Cedrus libani*)
16 Katsura tree (*Cercidiphyllum japonicum*)
17 Cedar (*Cedrus* spp.) grove of 7
18 Douglas fir (*Pseudotsuga menziesii*) 2
19 Shellbark hickory (*Carya laciniosa*)
20 American sweetgum (*Liquidambar styraciflua*) row of 5
21 Western larch (*Larix occidentalis*) *
22 American elm (*Ulmus americana*) row of 3
23 Smooth-leaf elm (*Ulmus carpinifolia*)
24 Chinese elm (*Ulmus parvifolia*)
25 Carolina poplar (*Populus* × *canadensis*) corner of 4
26 American sweetgum (*Liquidambar styraciflua*) row of 4
27 Ghost tree (*Acer negundo* 'Variegatum') 2
28 Japanese pagoda tree (*Sophora japonica*) 2
29 Lavalle hawthorn (*Crataegus* × *lavallei*)
30 Common horsechestnut (*Aesculus hippocastanum*)
31 Ginkgo (*Ginkgo biloba*)
32 Katsura tree (*Cercidiphyllum japonicum*) 2

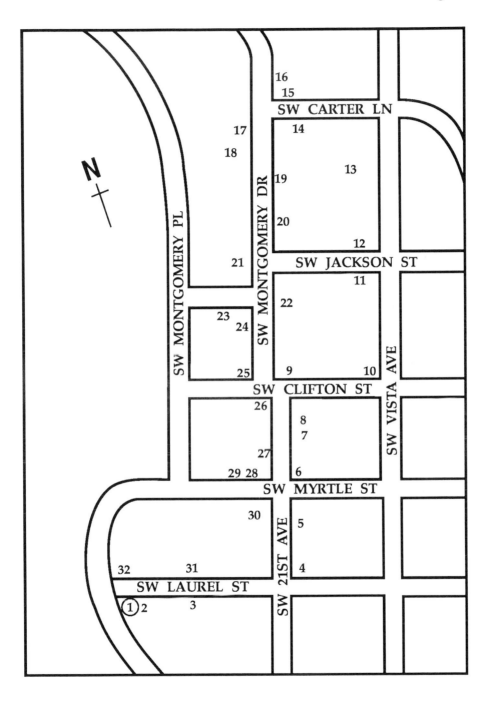

Reed College—Woodstock

Unitarian minister Thomas Lamb Eliot persuaded Amanda Reed to endow a college at the same time he persuaded the William Ladd family to donate 40 acres of cow pasture on their Crystal Springs farm for a campus. Contemporary with the college's origin is the plat of Eastmoreland, filed in 1910 and named for a real estate company official. Working with landscapers Lord and Schryver, Harvey Davis began collecting a thousand specimens for the Reed campus in the 1920s, and the Portland Garden Club set out a row of conifers along the campus on Woodstock in 1932. Nine holes of the Eastmoreland Public golf course were laid out in 1917 after Ladd donated the land. Aerial photos for 1953 show many of the present-day large trees as small specimens.

1 Western white pine (*Pinus monticola*)
2 Smooth-leaf elm (*Ulmus carpinifolia*)
3 English elm (*Ulmus procera*)
4 American sweetgum (*Liquidambar styraciflua*)
5 Northern red oak (*Quercus rubra*)
6 Port Orford cedar (*Chamaecyparis lawsoniana*) 3
7 Dutch elm (*Ulmus* × *hollandica*)
8 Giant sequoia (*Sequoiadendron giganteum*)
9 Ponderosa pine (*Pinus ponderosa*)
10 Scotch elm (*Ulmus glabra*)
11 Deodar (*Cedrus deodara*) 2
12 Incense cedar (*Calocedrus decurrens*) 2
13 Douglas fir (*Pseudotsuga menziesii*)
14 Canada hemlock (*Tsuga canadensis*)
15 Sitka spruce (*Picea sitchensis*)
16 Black locust (*Robinia pseudo-acacia*) grove of 5
17 Deodar (*Cedrus deodara*) 2
18 Copper beech (*Fagus sylvatica* 'Atropunicea') *

19 Port Orford cedar (*Chamaecyparis lawsoniana*) 3
20 Yellowwood (*Cladrastis lutea*) row of 5 *
21 Bigleaf linden (*Tilia platyphyllos*)
22 Northern red oak (*Quercus rubra*)
23 Japanese black pine (*Pinus thunbergiana*)
24 Japanese red pine (*Pinus densiflora*)
25 Variegated giant arborvitae (*Thuja plicata*) row of 25
26 Blue atlas cedar (*Cedrus atlantica* 'Glauca') 3
27 Atlas cedar (*Cedrus atlantica*)
28 Cedar of Lebanon (*Cedrus libani*)
29 Bristle-cone pine (*Pinus aristata*) group of 4
30 Giant sequoia (*Sequoiadendron giganteum*) group of 3
31 Western redcedar (*Thuja plicata*) grove of 5
32 Incense cedar (*Calocedrus decurrens*) row of 31
33 American elm (*Ulmus americana*) row of 11

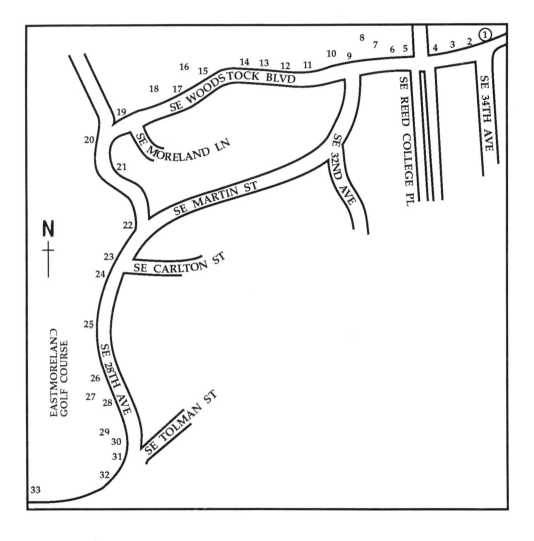

Sauvie Island

for bicyclists and motorists

The soils of Sauvie Island are often over 30 feet deep, built up by countless sediment deposits from the Columbia and Willamette rivers. Except for the annual or semi-annual floods that once plagued Sauvie Island, growing conditions made the island prime land for early settlers, who quickly filed their claims. At Fort William, the site of Nathaniel Wyeth's settlement of 1835, grafted fruit trees were first planted in the Oregon Territory.

To begin this tour, go to Sauvie Island Road. Just after circling off the bridge from US 30, you will see a sign on the left that reads, "Bybee Howell House, Game Mgt Area, Beaches, Sturgeon Lake." At the sign, set your odometer to 0 and continue 0.8 miles on Sauvie Island Road to Howell Park Road. Turn right.

Miles	Side	Tree
0.9	L	Scots pine (*Pinus sylvestris*)
0.9	R	Oregon white oak (*Quercus garryana*) 3
0.9	L	Japanese black pine (*Pinus thunbergiana*) 4
0.9	L	Lodgepole pine (*Pinus contorta*) 3
0.9	L	Eastern white pine (*Pinus strobus*)
0.9	L	Sweet cherry (*Prunus avium*)
0.9	L	Western redcedar (*Thuja plicata*)
0.9	L	Spanish chestnut (*Castanea sativa*)
0.9	L	Apple (*Malus* spp.) 2
0.9	L	English walnut (*Juglans regia*) 2
0.9	L	Pear (*Pyrus communis*)
1.3	—	Bigleaf maple (*Acer macrophyllum*) *

At 1.9 miles, turn right back on to Sauvie Island Road.

Miles	Side	Tree
2.9	R	Oregon white oak (*Quercus garryana*) 6
2.9	R	Coast redwood (*Sequoia sempervirens*)
3.1	R	Pin oak (*Quercus palustris*)
3.1	R	Red pine (*Pinus resinosa*)
3.2	R	Black walnut (*Juglans nigra*)
3.2	L	Western redcedar (*Thuja plicata*) grove
3.2	L	Pacific dogwood (*Cornus nuttallii*)
3.4	R	Oregon white oak (*Quercus garryana*)
4.0	L	Grand fir (*Abies grandis*)
4.0	L	Douglas fir (*Pseudotsuga menziesii*) grove
4.2	L	Silk tree (*Albizia julibrissin*)
4.3	R	Norway maple (*Acer platanoides*) row
4.4	L	Carolina poplar (*Populus × canadensis*)
4.6	R	Oregon white oak (*Quercus garryana*)
4.7	L	Northern red oak (*Quercus rubra*) grove
4.9	L	Oregon white oak (*Quercus garryana*) 2
5.3	L	Eastern redbud (*Cercis canadensis*) *
5.5	L	Black cottonwood (*Populus trichocarpa*) row
5.7	R	Oregon ash (*Fraxinus latifolia*)

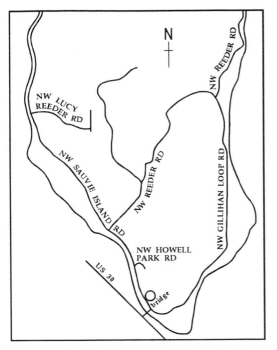

At 6.0 miles, turn right on to Lucy Reeder Road.

Miles	Side	Tree
6.6	R	Japanese flowering cherry (*Prunus serrulata*) (This grove is worth the trip only in early April.)

Return to Sauvie Island Road and go south (left turn) to Reeder Road. Reset the odometer to 0 at beginning of Reeder Road.

Miles	Side	Tree
0.1	R	Norway maple (*Acer platanoides*)
0.2	L	Japanese black pine (*Pinus thunbergiana*) 2
0.2	L	Lombardy poplar (*Populus nigra* 'Italica') 2
0.5	L	Norway maple (*Acer platanoides*) row
0.5	R	Deodar (*Cedrus deodara*)
0.9	R	Atlas cedar (*Cedrus atlantica*)
0.9	L&R	Oregon white oak (*Quercus garryana*) grove

Miles	Side	Tree
1.5	R	Weeping willow (*Salix babylonica*)
1.9	R	Oregon white oak (*Quercus garryana*)
2.0	R	Siberian elm (*Ulmus pumila*)
2.7	R	Littleleaf linden (*Tilia cordata*)
3.0	L	Coast redwood (*Sequoia sempervirens*)
3.1	L	Black cottonwood (*Populus trichocarpa*) row
4.4	R	Incense cedar (*Calocedrus decurrens*)
4.7	L	Weeping willow (*Salix babylonica*)
5.2	L	Black walnut (*Juglans nigra*)
5.2	R	Oregon ash (*Fraxinus latifolia*)
5.6	R	English walnut (*Juglans regia*) 2 *
5.7	R	Cascara (*Rhamnus purshiana*)
8.2	L	Black locust (*Robinia pseudoacacia*)

Turn around and go to start of Gillihan Road off Reeder Road. Set odometer to 0 at Gillihan Road.

Miles	Side	Tree
0.9	L	Weeping willow (*Salix babylonica*)
0.9	L	Chinese elm (*Ulmus parvifolia*)
0.9	L	Honey locust (*Gleditsia triacanthos*)
0.9	L	Chestnut (*Castanea* sp.)
0.9	L	Empress tree (*Paulownia tomentosa*) 5
1.0	L	Lombardy poplar (*Populus nigra* 'Italica')
1.0	L	Black walnut (*Juglans nigra*)
4.7	L	Spanish chestnut (*Castanea sativa*) 2
5.7	R	Weeping willow (*Salix babylonica*) *
6.3	end	(back where you started near the bridge)

Sellwood

The part of Sellwood encompassed by this walk originally belonged to the Henderson Luelling donation land claim and then was passed on to Joseph Lambert and Henry Miller. All three men were important pioneer tree people. Miller planted apple orchards on the land north of Nehalem Street, which he kept after the Rev. John Sellwood bought the portion to the south. In 1871 he moved into Portland where he became a florist and nursery owner.

When Sellwood was annexed into Portland in 1893, City View Park was platted west of 13th Avenue. Today Sellwood has some remarkable old trees, but records are scarce. Residents cared enough about their street trees to plant some unusual varieties in the parking strips. Look for streets lined with lindens, golden rain trees, and Raywood ashes.

1 Camperdown elm (*Ulmus* × *vegeta* 'Camperdownii')
2 Silver maple (*Acer saccharinum*) 3
3 Bigleaf maple (*Acer macrophyllum*)
4 Japanese snowbell (*Styrax japonicus*)
5 Common horsechestnut (*Aesculus hippocastanum*) 2
6 Mulberry (*Morus rubra*) group of 5
7 Deodar (*Cedrus deodara*)
8 European white birch (*Betula pendula* 'Dalecarlica')
9 Port Orford cedar (*Chamaecyparis lawsoniana*) row of 5
10 Bigleaf linden (*Tilia platyphyllos*)
11 Coast redwood (*Sequoia sempervirens*)
12 English walnut (*Juglans regia*)
13 Dawn redwood (*Metasequoia glyptostroboides*)
14 River birch (*Betula nigra*)
15 American sweetgum (*Liquidambar styraciflua*) 3
16 American sycamore (*Platanus occidentalis*)
17 White poplar (*Populus alba*)
18 Golden rain tree (*Koelreuteria paniculata*)
19 Raywood ash (*Fraxinus oxycarpa* 'Raywood') row of 6
20 Littleleaf linden (*Tilia cordata*) row of 5
21 Norway maple (*Acer platanoides*) 2
22 English hawthorn (*Crataegus laevigata*) 2
23 Ginkgo (*Ginkgo biloba*)
24 Western hemlock (*Tsuga heterophylla*)
25 Western redcedar (*Thuja plicata*)
26 Lodgepole pine (*Pinus contorta*)
27 Pissard's plum (*Prunus cerasifera* 'Atropurpurea') 2
28 Chinese chestnut (*Castanea mollissima*)
29 European mountain ash (*Sorbus aucuparia*) 2
30 American chestnut (*Castanea dentata*) 2 *
31 Colorado blue spruce (*Picea pungens*) 2

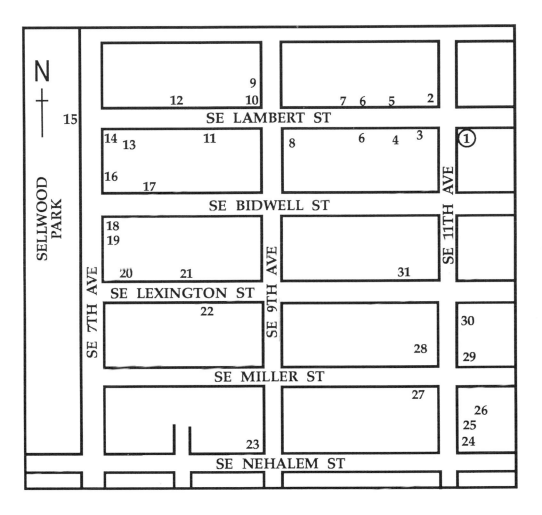

N

SELLWOOD PARK

15

9
12   10

7 6 5   2

SE LAMBERT ST

14 13   11

8   6   4   3

①

16
17

SE 11TH AVE

SE BIDWELL ST

18
19

20   21

31

SE 7TH AVE

SE 9TH AVE

SE LEXINGTON ST

22

30

28

29

SE MILLER ST

27

26
25
24

23

SE NEHALEM ST

South Park Blocks

In 1852 far-sighted planners platted 25 additional blocks to the city and created a strip of park land running north and south parallel to the city grid. Bordered by Park Avenue (8th) and West Park (9th), these blocks remained unimproved until 1876 when Louis Pfunder, a florist and nursery owner, planted lines of elms. Not everyone approved of the design. Harvey Scott wrote: "The trees in lines geometrically straight like an apple orchard [are] offensive to a man of sensitive taste" (quoted in O'Donnell and Vaughan 1976, 31). Scott preferred City [Washington] Park with its natural plantings but felt that had enough money been provided, City Park also would have been plowed and planted in geometric lines. Other elms were planted in the early 1900s to decorate the blocks in the fashion of European public lands. It is unfortunate that the line of park blocks was later broken by construction of buildings on the middle seven blocks. Listed are the trees of four blocks. This provides a representative sample of the species found in all of the south park blocks, from Salmon Street to Jackson Street.

1 Bigleaf linden (*Tilia platyphyllos*)
2 Lavalle hawthorn (*Crataegus* × *lavallei*)
3 London planetree (*Platanus* × *acerifolia*)

× European beech (*Fagus sylvatica*)
△ American elm (*Ulmus americana*)
□ European elm (*Ulmus* sp.)
○ Northern red oak (*Quercus rubra*)
♯ Sugar maple (*Acer saccharum*)

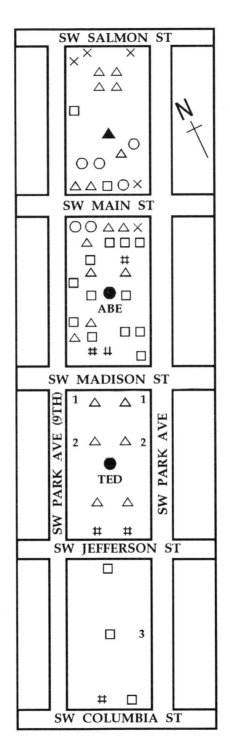

SE 37th and Steele

Just over one block long, this stretch of SE 37th Avenue presents an amazing collection of mature conifers. These trees were planted by Joseph A. Manning, a seed dealer and a connoisseur of unusual evergreens, who lived on this street in the early 1920s.

1 Coulter pine (*Pinus coulteri*) *
2 Western hemlock (*Tsuga heterophylla*)
3 Incense cedar (*Calocedrus decurrens*)
4 Engelmann spruce (*Picea engelmannii*)
5 Western hemlock (*Tsuga heterophylla*)
6 Giant sequoia (*Sequoiadendron giganteum*)
7 Monterey pine (*Pinus radiata*)
8 Incense cedar (*Calocedrus decurrens*)
9 Coast redwood (*Sequoia sempervirens*)
10 Coulter pine (*Pinus coulteri*)
11 Austrian pine (*Pinus nigra*)
12 Douglas fir (*Pseudotsuga menziesii*)
13 Norway spruce (*Picea abies*)

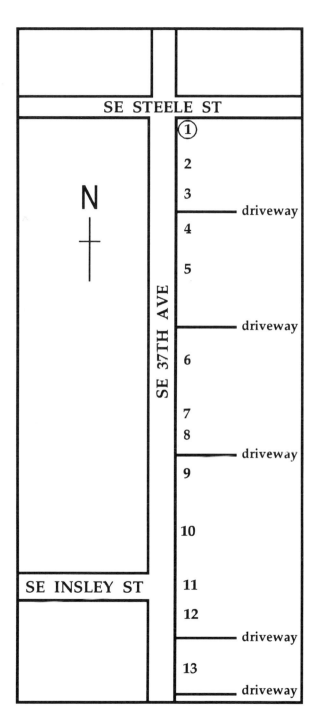

Largest Trees

Listed below are the 24 largest trees described in this volume. We arbitrarily chose a circumference of 200 inches (16'8") as the cutting off point.

336 in   *Acer macrophyllum* (Bigleaf maple)
12954 SW Howell Park Rd., Sauvie Island

303 in   *Platanus* × *acerifolia* (London planetree)
SE Stephens St. & 39th Ave.

300 in   *Sequoiadendron giganteum* (Giant sequoia)
1225 SE 60th Ave.

288 in   *Sequoiadendron giganteum* (Giant sequoia)
2174 SW Laurel St.

288 in   *Sequoiadendron giganteum* (Giant sequoia)
1728 SW Prospect Dr.

276 in   *Sequoiadendron giganteum* (Giant sequoia)
14105 SE River Rd., Milwaukie

276 in   *Sequoiadendron giganteum* (Giant sequoia)
2188 SW Main St.

260 in   *Sequoiadendron giganteum* (Giant sequoia)
5810 SE Taylor St.

252 in   *Populus nigra* 'Italica' (Lombardy poplar)
SE 17th Ave. & Taylor St.

252 in   *Acer macrophyllum* (Bigleaf maple)
6733 N Greeley Ave.

245 in   *Sequoia sempervirens* (Coast redwood)
812 SW Vista Ave.

232 in   *Quercus garryana* (Oregon white oak)
1815 N Humboldt St.

224 in   *Aesculus hippocastanum* (Common horsechestnut)
X 2045 SW 16th Ave.

222 in   *Acer macrophyllum* (Bigleaf maple)
NW 11th Dr. & Division St., Gresham

219 in   *Juglans nigra* (Black walnut)
X 17415 SW Walker Rd., Beaverton

219 in   *Fagus sylvatica* 'Atropunicea' (Copper beech)
SE Woodstock Blvd. near Moreland Ln., Reed College

216 in   *Quercus rubra* (Northern red oak)
1961 SW Vista Ave.

213 in   *Acer macrophyllum* (Bigleaf maple)
corner Monroe St. & 39th Ave., Milwaukie

211 in   *Fagus sylvatica* 'Atropunicea' (Purple beech)
1719 NE Knott St.

211 in   *Populus nigra* 'Italica' (Lombardy poplar)
4th St. between A & B Sts., Lake Oswego

208 in   *Platanus* × *acerifolia* (London planetree)
1816 SE 21st Ave.

208 in   *Fagus sylvatica* (European beech)
10115 NE Thompson St.

208 in   *Acer macrophyllum* (Bigleaf maple)
14170 SW Pacific Hwy., Tigard

201 in   *Juglans nigra* (Black walnut)
7101 SW Beaverton-Hillsdale Hwy.

Selected Bibliography

American Forestry Association. N.d. *National Register of Big Trees.* Washington, D. C.

Arno, S. F., and R. P. Hammerly. 1977. *Northwest Trees.* Seattle: The Mountaineers.

Bailey, L. H., and E. Z. Bailey. 1976. *Hortus Third.* Rev. by Staff of Liberty Hyde Bailey Horitorium. New York: MacMillan.

Bean, W. J. 1970. *Trees and Shrubs Hardy in the British Isles.* Vols. 1 & 2. 8th ed. Ed. G. Taylor. London: M. Bean & John Murray.

Brockman, C. F. 1968. *Trees of North America.* New York: Golden Press.

Brookfield, S. A. 1983. "Report on (Early Introduced) Pioneer Trees of Portland, Oregon." Unpublished paper. Portland: Oregon Historical Society.

Brown, J. E. 1982. "Identification Key to the Common Native Evergreen-Conifer Trees of Oregon." State of Oregon, Department of Forestry.

Cardwell, J. R. 1906. "A Brief History of Early Horticulture in Oregon." Unpublished paper. Portland: Oregon Historical Society.

Dallimore, W., and A. B. Jackson. 1966. *A Handbook of Coniferae and Ginkgoaceae.* Rev. by S. G. Harrison. London: Edward Arnold.

Davies, J. 1980. *Douglas of the Forests: the North American Journals of David Douglas.* Seattle: University of Washington Press.

Detling, L. E. 1968. "Historical Background of the Flora of the Pacific Northwest." University of Oregon Bulletin 13 (July).

Dirr, M. A. 1983. *Manual of Woody Landscape Plants.* 3rd ed. Champaign, IL: Stipes.

Drawson, M. 1974. *Treasures of the Oregon Country II.* Salem, OR: Dee.

Everett, T. H. 1981. *The New York Botanical Garden Illustrated Encyclopedia of Horticulture.* New York: Garland.

Florin, L. 1977. *Historic Glimpses of the Trees of the West.* Seattle: Superior.

The Garden Club of America. 1984. *Plants That Merit Attention.* Vol. 1, *Trees.* Ed. J. M. Poor. Portland, OR: Timber Press.

Garden Club of Amherst. 1975. *Trees in Amherst.* Amherst, MA: Garden Club of Amherst.

Hitchcock, C. L., and A. Cronquist. 1973. *Flora of the Pacific Northwest.* Seattle: University of Washington Press.

Jacobson, A. L. 1989. *Trees of Seattle.* Seattle: Sasquatch Books.

Kruckeberg, A. R. 1982. *Gardening with Native Plants of the Pacific Northwest.* Seattle: University of Washington Press.

Krüssmann, G. 1977. *Manual of Cultivated Broad-leaved Trees and Shrubs.* 3 vols. Trans. Michael E. Epp. Portland, OR: Timber Press.

———. 1983. *Manual of Cultivated Conifers.* Ed. Hans-Dieter Wards. Trans. Michael E. Epp. Portland, OR: Timber Press.

Lanzara, P., and M. Pizzetti. 1977. *Guide to Trees.* New York: Simon & Schuster.

Little, E. L., Jr. 1979. *Forest Trees of the United States and Canada, and How to Identify Them.* New York: Dover.

Miller, H. 1939. "Family MSS, Including Reminiscences of Franklin Miller." Historical Museum Collection, Milwaukie, OR.

Mitchell, A. 1987. *The Trees of North America.* New York: Facts on File.

Nisbet, R. A., Jr. 1979. "Early Horticulture in Oregon: Nurserymen and Pleasure Gardens." Paper for Philip Dole—Arch. 433. Eugene: University of Oregon.

O'Donnell, T., and T. Vaughan. 1976. *Portland: A Historical Sketch and Guide.* Portland: Oregon Historical Society.

Olson, C. O. 1965." History of Milwaukie, Oregon." (Unfinished MS prepared for the Federal Writer's Project of the Works Progress Administration). Historical Society, Milwaukie, OR.

Peattie, D. C. 1953. *A Natural History of Western Trees.* Boston: Houghton-Mifflin.

Portland City Council Records. 12 March 1987. Ordinance No. 134330. Title 20. Parks and Recreation.

———. 12 August 1982. Ordinance No. 153668. Title 33. Planning and Zoning.

Portland Park Board. 1903. *Annual Report.* Portland.

Rupp, R. 1990. *Red Oaks & Black Birches.* Pownal, VT: Garden Way, Storey Communications.

Spencer, O. C. 1950. *The Story of Sauvies Island.* Portland, OR: Binford and Mort.

Spongberg, S. H. 1990. *A Reunion of Trees.* Cambridge, MA: Harvard University Press.

Treseder, N. G. 1978. *Magnolias.* London: Faber & Faber.

Workers of the Writer's Program of the Works Progress Administration in the State of Oregon. 1940. *Oregon, End of the Trail.* Portland: Binford and Mort.

Glossary

Allée: a path or road defined by a row of trees (all the same species) on both sides.

Botanic name: the international scientific name assigned to a plant by taxonomists for classification and identification purposes. It is always composed of two words (both italicized), the first being the genus and the second the species.

Bract: a modified leaf, which may be of various colors, shapes, and consistencies and usually is associated with a flower.

Breed true: a seed is said to breed true if it reproduces a plant exactly like the parent. Some hybrids, cultivars, and varieties do not breed true and, therefore, must be propagated vegetatively.

Calyx (plural **calyces**): the collection (usually a fusion) of sepals in a flower.

Campanulate: bell-like.

Catkin: a spikelike inflorescence, often pendulous, composed of tiny flowers of only one sex.

Common name: the name a plant is known by in the lay (non-scientific) world. This name can vary from region to region and is, therefore, far less reliable than the botanic name for identification.

Compound leaf: a leaf composed of more than one blade or leaflet.

Compound ovary: the female part of a plant with two or more ovules.

Conifer: a cone-bearing or, in a very few instances, berry-bearing, needled or scalelike foliaged tree or shrub. *Ginkgo biloba* is the only conifer with leaves that are not shaped like needles or scales.

Cultivar: a horticultural variety that has originated and persisted under cultivation. Cultivar names are English, not Latin.

Cuttings: portions removed (cut) from a plant's stem or root used for vegetative propagation purposes.

Cyme: a broad, flat inflorescence in which the outer flowers are the last to open.

Espalier: to train a plant to grow on a trellis or framework.

Foliage: leaves.

Genus (plural **genera**): a group of related species; the first word in the botanic name, the first letter always capitalized; always in italics, and in Latin.

Grafting: a method of plant propagation whereby one kind of plant, often a branch, is attached onto another closely related kind. There are several grafting methods.

Hybrid: a plant resulting from a cross between parents that are genetically unlike, most often between two different species.

Inflorescence: a flower cluster.

Introduce: to bring a non-native plant to a new region where it will be either sold by the nursery trade or privately grown and, most likely, propagated.

Layering: rooting of a branch that is still connected to the tree or shrub.

Leader: the primary or terminal shoot of a tree.

Lobe: a large projecting segment of the margin of a leaf.

Midrib: the main rib of a leaf, a continuation of the petiole.

Mutant: hereditary change in a plant with visible effect. Vegetative propagation is often the only means of maintaining plants of mutant origin.

Native: originating naturally in a particular region.

Naturalize: to introduce plants into a region where they flourish as if native.

Node: a joint on a stem, usually where a leaf or bud arises.

Ovule: the part of a plant that, after fertilization, becomes the seed.

Panicle: an elongate inflorescence of clusters, where the oldest (first-blooming) flower clusters are at the base. Bloom is successive toward the tip.

Petiole: leaf stalk. The part that attaches the leaf to the branch.

Pollarded: a tree cut back nearly to the trunk so as to produce a dense new growth of branches. Pollarding is often done to control height and spread.

Pome: a type of fleshy fruit of the rose family resulting from a compound ovary (e.g., an apple; pomelike, therefore, means applelike).

Raceme: an elongate inflorescence cluster with the older flowers (simple) at the base and the younger flowers at the tip.

Racemose: having flowers in racemes.

Rhizome: a horizontal underground stem.

Rootstock: the root used by plant propagators for grafting cultivars. Often a rootstock will have qualities that enhance good growth.

Scion: a detached portion of a plant consisting of more than one bud, capable of propagation.

Secondary branches: smaller branches extending from the main branches.

Sepal: the outermost (toward the stem) whorl of the flower parts, usually green, but on some plants colored and resembling petals.

Serrate: toothed, as along the edge of a leaf, with the teeth pointing forward.

Sessile: without a stalk.

Silver thaw: a local term for freezing rain when, due to rapidly falling temperature, rain quickly becomes ice that heavily coats everything. The weight of the ice can cause limbs and sometimes trunks of trees to break. The ice storm is stopped by the arrival of a warm west wind called a Chinook.

Sinus: the concave space between two leaf lobes.

Species (plural also **species**): a group of plants (or animals) that shares attributes and interbreeds.

Species name: in the botanic name of a plant, it is the second word, non-capitalized, and always in italics and Latin. This word can be derived from such sources as a person's name, an attribute of the plant, the plant's native habitat.

Specific name: another way of saying species name (the adjectival form).

Suckers: fast-growing shoots that grow (usually in a vertical direction) from roots, trunks, or branches of trees. Not all trees produce suckers.

Taxon (plural **taxa**): a recognized group of organisms of any rank in a classification hierarchy (e.g., class, order, family, genus, species).

Taxonomist: a person occupied in the science of identifying, naming, and classifying organisms.

Toothed leaf: a leaf edge that has regular, toothlike indentations.

Vegetative propagation: production of offspring from cuttings, layerings, stolons, or rhizomes.

Index of Tree Names

Abies
    concolor 24, 175, 187, 188
    grandis 25, 175, 186, 192
    pinsapo 26, 175
    procera 27, 175, 186
Acer
    campestre 28, 177, 184
    circinatum 15, 184
    macrophyllum 15, 29–31, 177, 179,
        182, 184, 192, 194, 201, 202
    negundo 'Variegatum' 32, 177, 182,
        188
    palmatum 33, 177, 179, 184
    platanoides 34, 35, 176, 179, 184,
        192, 193, 194
    platanoides 'Harlequin' 34
    pseudoplatanus 35, 176, 182, 184
    rubrum 36, 176, 179
    saccharinum 37, 176, 182, 184, 194
    saccharum 38, 179, 182, 196
Aesculus
    glabra 39, 179
    hippocastanum 40, 42, 57, 177, 182,
        188, 194, 202
    octandra 41, 177, 179
    pavia 42
    × *carnea* 42, 177
Ailanthus altissima 43, 178, 179
Albizia julibrissin 44, 178, 179, 182,
    184, 186, 192
Apple 192
    lady 187
    'Yellow Bellflower' 106
Araucaria araucana 19, 45, 175, 182
Arborvitae
    giant 159, 190
Arbutus menziesii 10, 46–47, 175, 177,
    179, 184

Ash
    European mountain 194
    Oregon 82, 178, 179, 192, 193
    Raywood 194
Aspen
    quaking 129, 180

Bay
    European 172
Beech
    copper 80–81, 190, 202
    European 80, 177, 196, 202
    purple 80–81, 182, 202
Betula
    nigra 48, 177, 179, 194
    papyrifera 49, 177, 179
    pendula 50, 177, 179, 184, 188
    pendula 'Dalecarlica' 50, 182, 194
Birch
    European white 50, 177, 179, 184,
        188
    European white 'Dalecarlica' 50,
        182, 194
    paper 49, 177, 179
    river 48, 177, 179, 194
Boxelder
    green 32
    variegated 32
Buckeye
    Ohio 39, 179
    yellow 41, 177, 179

Calocedrus decurrens 51, 175, 184, 190,
    193, 198
Carpinus
    betulus 52, 178
    caroliniana 53, 178

Carya
  laciniosa 188
  ovata 54, 179, 184
  tomentosa 55, 179
Cascara 193
Castanea 193
  dentata 56, 57, 178, 194
  mollissima 194
  sativa 56, 57, 178, 186, 192, 193
Castanopsis chrysophylla 15
Catalpa
  bignonioides 58, 175, 178
  speciosa 59, 178, 184, 186, 187
Catalpa
  Northern 59, 178, 184, 186, 187
  Southern 58, 175, 178
Cedar 188
  Alaska 66, 160, 175, 184
  atlas 60–61, 175, 187, 190, 193
  blue atlas 60–61, 186, 190
  deodar 60–61, 175, 182, 184, 186,
    187, 190, 193, 194
  Hogan 160
  incense 51, 175, 184, 190, 193, 198
  Japanese 74
  of Lebanon 18, 60–61, 175, 188,
    190
  Port Orford 64–65, 66, 160, 175,
    182, 184, 186, 190, 194
  Western red 64, 159–160, 176, 182,
    184, 190, 192, 194
Cedrus 188
  atlantica 60–61, 175, 187, 190, 193
  atlantica 'Glauca' 60–61, 186, 190
  deodara 60–61, 175, 182, 184, 186,
    187, 190, 193, 194
  libani 60–61, 175, 188, 190
Cercidiphyllum japonicum 62, 177, 179,
  188
Cercis canadensis 63, 177, 186, 192
Chamaecyparis
  lawsoniana 64–65, 175, 182, 184,
    186, 190, 194
  nootkatensis 66, 175, 184
Cherry
  Akebono 136
  Bing 18, 132–133
  Japanese flowering 135–136, 176,
    193
  Kwanzan 135, 177
  Mt. Fuji 136
  Mazzard 132
  Royal Ann 132–133, 176
  Shirotae 136

  sweet 132, 177, 192
  weeping Japanese 137, 176
  wild 15
Chestnut 193
  American 56, 178, 194
  Chinese 56, 194
  European 57
  horse 40, 42, 57, 177, 182, 188, 194,
    202
  Spanish 57, 178, 186, 192, 193
Chinquapin
  golden 15
Cladrastis lutea 67, 177, 184, 190
Clerodendrum trichotomum 68, 178,
  179
Cornus
  florida 69, 177, 179
  nuttallii 10, 70–71, 177, 179, 184,
    192
Corylus cornuta 15
Cottonwood
  black 130, 180, 192, 193
  Eastern 131
Crabapple
  Japanese flowering 105, 176
  Oregon 15
  purple 107
Crapemyrtle 91, 179
Crataegus
  douglasii 15
  laevigata 72, 177, 194
  × *lavallei* 73, 177, 179, 188, 196
Cryptomeria 74, 175
Cryptomeria japonica 74, 175
Cucumber tree 98, 177
Cunninghamia lanceolata 75, 175
Cupressocyparis leylandii 182
Cypress
  Leyland 182
  sawara 24

Davidia involucrata 76–77, 177
Dawn redwood 108–109, 177, 179,
  182, 186, 194
Deodar 60–61, 175, 182, 184, 186,
  187, 190, 193, 194
Diospyros 186
  kaki 78, 179
  virginiana 78
Dogwood
  Eastern 69
  flowering 69, 177, 179
  Pacific 10, 70–71, 177, 179, 184,
    192

Western 70–71
Douglas fir 15, 138–139, 176, 184, 186, 188, 190, 198
Dove tree 76–77, 177

Elm
    Abernethy 165
    American 165–167, 178, 188, 190, 196
    Burrell 167
    Camperdown 171, 194
    Chinese 169, 178, 188, 193
    Dutch 190
    English 170, 178, 182, 188, 190
    European 165, 186, 188, 196
    New world 181
    Old world 181
    Scotch 168, 190
    Siberian 193
    smooth-leaf 182, 188, 190
    variegated English 170
    Washington 19, 166
    wych 168
Empress tree 112, 177, 186, 193
Eriobotrya japonica 79, 175, 180

Fagus
    sylvatica 80–81, 177, 196, 202
    sylvatica 'Atropunicea' 80–81, 182, 190, 202
Fir
    China 75, 175
    Douglas 15, 138–139, 176, 184, 186, 188, 190, 198
    grand 25, 175, 186, 192
    noble 27, 175, 186
    Spanish 26, 175
    white 24, 175, 187, 188
Fraxinus
    latifolia 82, 178, 179, 192, 193
    oxycarpa 'Raywood' 194

Ghost tree 32, 177, 182, 188
Ginkgo 19, 83–84, 177, 179, 182, 188, 194
Ginkgo biloba 83–84, 177, 179, 182, 188, 194, 205
Gleditsia
    triacanthos 85, 193
    triacanthos var. *inermis* 85, 177
Glory bower 68, 178, 179
Golden chaintree 90, 177
Golden chinquapin 15
Golden rain tree 89, 177, 178, 179, 194

Gum
    black 110
    sour 110

Handkerchief tree 76–77
Harlequin 68
Hawthorn
    Carriere 73
    Douglas 15
    English 72, 177, 194
    Lavalle 73, 177, 179, 188, 196
Hazel
    Western 15
Hemlock
    Canada 190
    Western 164, 176, 184, 194, 198
Hickory
    mockernut 55, 179
    shagbark 54, 179, 184
    shellbark 188
Hogan cedar 160
Honeylocust
    common 85, 193
    thornless common 85
Hornbeam
    American 53, 178
    European 52, 178
Horsechestnut
    common 40, 57, 177, 182, 188, 194, 202
    red 42, 177
Hydrangea
    panicle 86, 179
Hydrangea paniculata 86, 179

Incense cedar 51, 175, 184, 190, 193, 198

Juniper
    California 187
Juniperus californica 187
Juglans
    nigra 87, 177, 182, 186, 192, 193, 202
    regia 88, 177, 182, 184, 192, 193, 194

Katsura tree 62, 177, 179, 188
Koelreuteria paniculata 89, 177, 178, 179, 194

Laburnum anagyroides 90, 177
Laegerstroemia indica 91, 179

Larch 60, 108
    European 92, 176, 179
    Japanese 93, 176, 179
    Western 94, 176, 179, 188
Larix
    decidua 92, 176, 179
    kaempferi 93, 176, 179
    occidentalis 94, 176, 179, 188
Laurel
    California 172, 176, 184
Laurus nobilis 172
Linden 162
    bigleaf 161, 178, 186, 190, 194, 196
    little-leaf 193, 194
    silver 162, 178
Liquidambar styraciflua 95, 179, 182,
    188, 190, 194
Liriodendron tulipifera 96–97, 177, 179,
    182, 184
Locust
    black 148, 178, 184, 190, 193
    honey 85, 193
Loquat 79, 175, 180

Madrona 46–47
Madrone
    Pacific 10, 46–47, 175, 177, 179,
        184
Magnolia
    acuminata 98, 177
    dawsoniana 99, 176
    denudata 100, 104, 176
    grandiflora 101, 175, 178, 179, 182
    sargentiana var. *robusta* 102, 176
    tripetala 103, 178
    × *soulangiana* 104, 176, 182
Magnolia
    Dawson's 99, 176
    Sargent 102, 176
    saucer 104, 176, 182
    Southern 101, 175, 178, 179, 182
    umbrella 103, 178
    Yulan 100, 176
Maidenhair tree 83–84
Malus 187, 192
    floribunda 105, 176
    pumila 'Yellow Bellflower' 106
    × *purpurea* 107
Maple
    bigleaf 15, 29–31, 35, 177, 179, 182,
        184, 192, 194, 201, 202
    field 28
    hedge 28, 177, 184
    Japanese 33, 177, 179, 184

    Norway 28, 34, 35, 176, 179, 184,
        192, 193, 194
    Pow-wow 18, 30
    red 36, 176, 179
    silver 37, 176, 182, 184, 194
    sugar 38, 179, 182, 196
    sycamore 35, 176, 182, 184
    vine 15, 184
Metasequoia glyptostroboides 108–109,
    177, 179, 182, 186, 194
Mitten tree 151
Monkey puzzle 19, 45, 175, 182
Morus rubra 194
Mulberry 194
Myrtle
    Oregon 172

Nyssa sylvatica 110, 179

Oak
    black 146
    bur 187
    English 182
    Garry 10, 143–144
    Northern red 146, 178, 180, 184,
        188, 190, 192, 196, 202
    Oregon white 10, 15, 143–144,
        176, 178, 186, 187, 192, 193, 202
    pin 145, 178, 180, 182, 184, 192
    scarlet 187
    Strong 143–144
    swamp white 142, 178
Oxydendrum arboreum 111, 180

Pagoda tree
    Japanese 156, 178, 179, 188
Palm
    Chinese windmill 163, 176
Paulownia 112
Paulownia tomentosa 112, 177, 186, 193
Pear 141, 176, 180, 192
    callery 140, 176, 180
    callery 'Chanticleer' 140
Persimmon 186
    American 78
    Japanese 78, 179
Photinia
    Chinese 113, 177
Photinia serrulata 113, 177
Picea
    abies 114, 175, 188, 198
    breweriana 115, 175
    engelmannii 187, 198
    pungens 116, 175, 182, 187, 194

sitchensis 117, 176, 184, 186, 190
Pine
    Austrian 18, 122, 176, 184, 198
    big-cone 119
    bristlecone 190
    coast 118
    Coulter 119, 176, 198
    Eastern white 186, 192
    Japanese black 190, 192, 193
    Japanese red 120, 176, 190
    lodgepole 118, 176, 184, 192, 194
    Monterey 198
    pitch 119
    ponderosa 10, 123–124, 176, 184,
        186, 187, 190
    red 192
    shore 118
    Scots 192
    Tanyosho 120
    umbrella 152, 176, 182
    Western white 121, 176, 190
Pinus
    aristata 190
    contorta 118, 176, 184, 192, 194
    coulteri 119, 176, 198
    densiflora 120, 176, 190
    monticola 121, 176, 190
    nigra 122, 176, 184, 198
    ponderosa 10, 123–124, 176, 184,
        186, 187, 190
    radiata 198
    resinosa 192
    strobus 186, 192
    sylvestris 192
    thunbergiana 190, 192, 193
Planetree 34
    American 125, 177, 182, 194
    London 125, 126–127, 178, 182,
        196, 201, 202
    Oriental 126
Platanus
    occidentalis 125, 126, 177, 182, 194
    orientalis 126
    × *acerifolia* 126–127, 178, 182, 196,
        201, 202
Plum
    European 134, 176
    Pissard's 182, 194
Poplar
    Carolina 131, 178, 180, 188, 192
    Lombardy 128, 131, 180, 188, 193,
        201, 202
    white 194
    yellow 96–97

Populus
    alba 194
    deltoides 131
    nigra 'Italica' 128, 131, 180, 188,
        193, 201, 202
    tremuloides 129, 180
    trichocarpa 130, 180, 192, 193
    × *canadensis* 131, 178, 180, 188, 192
Prunus
    avium 132–133, 135, 177, 192
    avium 'Bing' 132–133
    avium 'Royal Ann' 132–133, 176
    cerasifera 'Atropurpurea' 182, 194
    domestica 134, 176
    emarginata var. *mollis* 15
    serrulata 135–136, 176, 193
    serrulata 'Akebono' 136
    serrulata 'Kwanzan' 135, 177
    serrulata 'Mt. Fuji' 136
    serrulata 'Shirotae' 136
    subhirtella 'Pendula' 137, 176
Pseudotsuga menziesii 15, 138–139,
    176, 184, 186, 188, 190, 198
Pterocarya fraxinifolia 182
Pyrus
    calleryana 140, 176, 180
    calleryana 'Chanticleer' 140
    communis 141, 176, 180, 192
    fusca 15

Quercus
    bicolor 142, 178
    coccinea 187
    garryana 10, 15, 143–144, 176, 178,
        186, 187, 192, 193, 202
    macrocarpa 187
    palustris 145, 178, 180, 182, 184,
        192
    robur 182
    rubra 146, 178, 180, 184, 188, 190,
        192, 196, 202
    velutina 146

Redbud
    Eastern 63, 177, 186, 192
    Western 63
Redcedar
    Hogan 160
    Western 64, 159–160, 176, 182,
        184, 190, 192, 194
Redwood
    coast 153, 176, 182, 184, 186, 187,
        192, 193, 194, 198, 201
    dawn 108–109, 177, 179, 182, 186,
        194

Rhamnus purshiana 193
Rhododendron 147, 178
Rhododendron ponticum 147, 178
Robinia pseudoacacia 148, 178, 184, 190, 193

Salix
   babylonica 149, 176, 193
   matsudana 'Tortuosa' 150, 176
Sassafras 151, 180, 186
Sassafras albidum 151, 180, 186
Scholar tree
   Chinese 156
Sciadopytis verticillata 152, 176, 182
Sequoia
   giant 10, 18–19, 154–155, 160, 176, 184, 186, 187, 188, 190, 198, 201
Sequoia sempervirens 153, 154, 176, 182, 184, 186, 187, 192, 193, 194, 198, 201
Sequoiadendron giganteum 10, 19, 154–155, 176, 184, 186, 187, 188, 190, 198, 201
Silk tree 44, 178, 179, 182, 184, 186, 192
Snowbell
   Japanese 157, 178, 180, 194
Sophora japonica 156, 178, 179, 188
Sorbus aucuparia 194
Sourwood 111, 180
Spruce
   Brewer 115, 175
   Colorado 116, 175, 182, 187, 194
   Engelmann 187, 198
   Norway 24, 114, 175, 188, 198
   Sitka 117, 176, 184, 186, 190
Styrax japonicus 157, 178, 180, 194
Sweetgum
   American 95, 179, 182, 188, 190, 194
Sycamore 34, 35, 125
   American 125
   Farrell 127

Tamarack 94
Tamarisk 158, 177, 184
Tamarix parviflora 158, 177, 184
Taxus brevifolia 158

Thuja plicata 159–160, 176, 182, 184, 190, 192, 194
Tilia
   cordata 193, 194
   platyphyllos 161, 178, 186, 190, 194, 196
   tomentosa 162, 178
Trachycarpus fortunei 163, 176
Tree of heaven 43, 178, 179
Tsuga
   canadensis 190
   heterophylla 164, 176, 184, 194, 198
Tulip tree 96–97, 177, 179, 182, 184
Tupelo 110, 179

Ulmus 181, 186, 188, 196
   americana 165–167, 178, 188, 190, 196
   carpinifolia 182, 188, 190
   glabra 168, 190
   parvifolia 169, 178, 188, 193
   procera 170, 178, 182, 188, 190
   procera 'Argento-variegata' 170
   pumila 193
   × *hollandica* 190
   × *vegeta* 'Camperdownii' 171, 194
Umbellularia californica 172, 176, 184
Umbrella pine 152, 176, 182

Walnut
   black 87, 177, 182, 186, 192, 193, 202
   English 88, 177, 182, 184, 192, 193, 194
Willow
   corkscrew 150, 176
   weeping 149, 176, 193
Wingnut
   Caucasian 182

Yellowwood 67, 177, 184, 190
Yew
   Western 158

Zelkova
   Japanese 173, 178, 180
Zelkova serrata 173, 178, 180

About the Authors

Photo by Marie Hall Steinberg.

A native of Portland whose long-term interest in trees leads her to propagate them from seed, Phyllis C. Reynolds (*photo right*) has lived in the city for 40 years. She has written several articles about trees and shrubs, including one on the pleasures and tribulations of plant identification in Japan, and has served on the board and the tree acquisition committee for the Hoyt Arboretum Friends Foundation and the boards of the Japanese Garden Society and the Berry Botanic Garden. A retired clinical psychologist and an artist, Dr. Reynolds has exhibited monotypes and etchings at several galleries in the Pacific Northwest.

Elizabeth F. Dimon (*photo left*), also a native of Portland, was an avid historian and expert gardener prior to her death in 1991. Author of "Twas Many Years Since," a history of the Waverley Heights neighborhood where she lived, and a paper on Henderson Luelling, the early Oregon horticulturist, Ms. Dimon served on the board of the Oregon Historical Society and was chair of its publication committee. She was also on the boards of the Society of Colonial Dames of Oregon, the Milwaukie Historical Society, McLoughlin House in

Oregon City, and the Hoover-Minthorn House in Newberg, and was active in the Portland Garden Club and the Home Orchard Society.

Friends since high school at Catlin School (now Catlin Gabel School), the authors hope that this book will keep many of Portland's beautiful and historic trees alive for future generations to see and enjoy.